CONTRADICTIONS

Notes on Twenty-six Years in the Theatre

HAL PRINCE

CONTRADICTIONS

Notes on Twenty-six Years
in the Theatre

ILLUSTRATED WITH PHOTOGRAPHS

DODD, MEAD & COMPANY

NEW YORK

ISBN: 0-396-07019-1
Library of Congress Catalog Card Number: 74-10399

Printed in the United States of America
by The Cornwall Press, Cornwall, N.Y.

For Judy,
a snob about the theatre

INTRODUCTION

I get a lot of mail from theatre enthusiasts, many of them in universities, some, unbelievable as it may seem, still in the lower schools, with questions about the creative and business areas of the theatre today. I've worked almost exclusively on Broadway or on touring companies of plays which originated on Broadway, so the questions usually apply to Broadway theatre.

Though my work in New York has been predominantly on musicals, most of my opinions apply equally to plays without music, just as, surprisingly, most of the questions I receive extend to non-musical theatre.

The most popular and least possible question to answer by mail is: "What is producing?" It is generally followed by: "What is the difference between the producer and the director?" I have a form letter for those questions, and the more specific and stimulating ones I answer individually.

The last couple of years my mail has tripled, and this year my letters often come from people who are doing doctorates on theatre and contain dozens of questions.

This book, then, grows out of my desire to cut down on my mail.

Also, I've been working in New York since 1948, and this is as good a time as any to take some stock and come to some conclusions with respect to the way the theatre is going and just how invalided the theatre is. And perhaps more personally what my future in the theatre might hold. So in collating all these questions and asking more, I've come to some conclusions, ordered out of chaos the tangle of information, of experience, of surprises and disappointments, frustrations.

I've had a unique life in the theatre, uniquely lucky. I went to work for George Abbott in 1948, and I was fired one Friday that year from a television job in his office. I was rehired the following Monday, and I've never been out of work since. Perhaps Neil Simon's play *The Prisoner of Second Avenue* got to me as profoundly as it did because the leading character came home one day and announced that he'd lost his job. I suppose I'll always live in unreasonable lunatic fear of losing my job.

So this book grew out of hundreds of letters written and a dialogue between me and Annette Meyers, who has been my secretary and my assistant and something of a devil's advocate for fourteen years. She came to my office an English teacher from New Jersey. She has learned just about everything there is to know about how we do our shows, and she has seen the theatre enter this confusing and harrowing period of change (which I hope is documented in the text to follow). She is married to an actor-writer, which means that she is probably privy to information and attitudes to which it would be difficult for me to be exposed.

This familiarity with the other side—a term I deplore because the lines which separate and departmentalize the theatre are taking a terrible toll on it, particularly today— has qualified her to frame some of these questions in a way that has caused me to look at aspects of the theatre that I generally ignore.

There are very few anecdotes in this book and a modicum of names get dropped. It isn't glamorous, because I don't think the theatre is—not in terms of diamonds and sable. People lament that fact, but I think it is neither to lament nor to celebrate. Times have changed and the theatre with them.

To simplify things, I have presented the material in chronological order, starting with something about myself and then launching into the twenty shows. I have taken them one by one, and in the course of each one I have tried to analyze what I learned, first at George Abbott's elbow and then at Jerome Robbins', and then at all those other collective elbows, the authors', composers', lyricists', designers', choreographers', the actors', and the company managers'. The first of the shows is *The Pajama Game,* the most recent, *Candide.*

The first version of this book covered 650 pages. I have eliminated everything about each show which was routine—operational redundancies. What remains is what remains interesting to me in the continuing learning process which is "doing" plays. And, hopefully, in what remains are answers to most of the questions I am asked.

The book dictated its own title. We started it three and a half years ago, and about halfway through Annette began to collect instances in which I changed my mind totally, reversed myself a hundred eighty degrees. I have a predilection for oversimplifying. It makes my life more pleasant. I am an optimist—which also makes my life more pleasant. Annette Meyers enjoys threshing up the contradictions and she endures pessimism. Somewhere, probably, between the two of us exists a measure of reality.

Contradictions as such don't bother me too much (what is it Emerson said?). The only one from which there seems no respite—*the ultimate contradiction*—is born of my desire to work ALL THE TIME and my fear of working just to keep busy.

I don't know.

CONTRADICTIONS

Notes on Twenty-six Years in the Theatre

CHAPTER 1

We were privileged, upper-middle lower-rich class, Jewish, both parents of German families which settled here soon after the Civil War. There was never any question that I would go to college, that I would travel, that I would go to the theatre early and often. Mine was a family addicted to theatre, and still there was no effort to encourage me to work in it nor to discourage me, and at no time was there any to push me into finance. So I didn't have to resist something I *would* have resisted.

I was always preparing myself for this. I fantasized a lot as a kid; most kids do. Some kids don't, but I did. And my fantasies took the shape of the life I'm living now. How many people can say that?

I've had theatre ambitions all of my life. I cannot go back so far that I don't remember where I wanted to work. The only difference is that what I wanted to be was a playwright, and that still stands me in good stead. But I am not a playwright.

Saturday matinees were part of a New York Jewish

child's intellectual upbringing. I spent mine in the orchestra with my parents or up in the top balcony of the Empire Theatre with a school friend or by myself. My allowance went for theatre tickets rather than ball games, and I saw Orson Welles when he was twenty-one do *Julius Caesar*, Burgess Meredith in *Winterset*, Bankhead in *The Little Foxes*, Schildkraut and Le Gallienne together in *Uncle Harry*, not great, just marvelous. I saw the usual kid stuff: *White Horse Inn*; I saw *The American Way*; I saw something called *In Old Virginia* at the Center Theatre and there was a sequence in which a whale swallowed Jonah. I thought that was something.

I wasn't as interested in musicals, and by the time I got to the University of Pennsylvania, I wasn't interested in them at all.

I ran a radio station which I had helped form at the University, writing weekly adaptations of plays, pirating everything: O'Neill, Maxwell Anderson, Odets, and so on, and I would direct those and act in them sometimes.

Also, I wanted to be a novelist. I wrote novels beginning early in my teens and continuing through college. I remember working at a Smith-Corona portable till four or five every morning. In that period I wrote four novels and as many full-length plays. I wish I knew what became of all that material. Just to see.

I was not a drama major. There was no such thing. And I don't believe in it. I don't approve. Everything theatrical at Penn was extracurricular. I took a liberal arts course: English, psychology, heavy on history (still my favorite subject), philosophy, and I read plays—many plays. I think it's fine to study drama if you want to be a scholar, a critic, to teach. I do not think you get much valuable, practical experience in college dramatic programs. Maybe they are getting more practical and less self-congratulatory, less social, but I think probably on a postgraduate level.

I was a fair student. I went to college when I was barely sixteen and finished when I was still nineteen. Too fast, I think, but to compensate I came to appreciate that I had gotten the beat on my peers. I was working for George Abbott when I was twenty.

I never believed in the apprenticeship system, so I never tried summer stock. I don't think that kids going to Westport, putting on blue jeans and oxford shirts, and splattering paint all over themselves are learning a damn thing about the theatre. They're learning what a lot of fun Arlene Francis is and what a lot of fun you can have in Westport, Connecticut, during the summer. There's nothing tidy, comfortable, social about the experience of learning your craft in the theatre.

I was very bad about looking for work. I was shy and as silent as I am presently loquacious, so I fooled myself into thinking I was "making the rounds" by writing plays and having *them* make the rounds instead. One of these reached the desk of the head of the script department at ABC-TV. He had heard that George Abbott was organizing a small experimental TV unit and arranged an interview for me with someone in the Abbott office. I went straight over there, and I never left. We still share an office, and it is only across the street from the one I entered twenty-six years ago.

At the time of the Abbott office interview, I remember I said I could not imagine what I could do to earn even

$25 a week, so I offered to work "on spec" for nothing. I offered to leave at any point if they discerned in the quality of my work that I was not being paid. That amused somebody, and I went to work for nothing. Two weeks later I was raised to $25 a week, and I stayed at that figure for six months.

I did a little of everything. We soon had three shows on television, the most prestigious of them, *The Hugh Martin Show,* an original musical, which George Abbott wrote, featuring Joan McCracken and Hugh Martin, the Hugh Martin Singers, Butterfly McQueen, and Kaye Ballard. It supposedly took place in Hugh Martin's living room. It was modest. It appeared on NBC Sunday nights at seven. Abbott wrote the first one and directed it, and then he let me write the second and direct it. He simply approved what I was doing and went away and let me do it. Soon I got into a battle with Kaye Ballard, the comedienne on the show. I was a nervous kid in those days, nervous, ambitious, apprehensive. It was irritating to observe how quickly I moved, how intensely I worked. After all, you never know when someone's watching. We clashed, and Hugh Martin, who had brought Kaye into the show and was a great friend of hers, went to Abbott and insisted I be taken off the show, and Abbott refused. Martin put it to Abbott: Prince or the show. Abbott chose Prince; the show went off the air.

Actually the television operation annoyed Abbott for many good reasons. There was so much activity; many shows on the air, much hysteria in the office (Abbott prefers CALM), and no money coming in—a poor combination. So one Friday Abbott disbanded the television department.

It was three in the afternoon, and I went straight to what is now the DeMille Theatre on Broadway where I sat in a cold sweat till well past midnight. I'd lost the best job in New York.

On Monday morning, when I went back to empty my desk, Bobby Griffith, who was George Abbott's production stage manager, told Abbott that he'd been unhappy for some time with his assistant and requested he replace him with me. So I had a new job, and it paid $75 a week. The show, a revue called *Touch and Go*, had originated at Catholic University in Washington, D.C., and was written by Jean and Walter Kerr.

Everything began to move quickly. I worked nights as second assistant stage manager at the Broadhurst and days in the Abbott office, running the switchboard, casting, messengering—the works. And there was a show in Boston called *Tickets, Please* with Paul and Grace Hartman which was in some trouble. Its director had been fired and Abbott called in. Abbott wanted a stage manager to take with him to Boston, and as Bobby Griffith was in London, staging an edition of *Touch and Go*, I went to Boston, where I became first assistant stage manager and where I met the Hartmans.

Nights I worked on their show and days I wrote a play with Ted Luce, who had written much of the *Tickets, Please* material.

The show ran a season, and by the end of its run, Ted and I had written a comedy-murder mystery called *A Perfect Scream,* and the Hartmans had optioned it, and I joined the Dramatists Guild. (The Hartmans separated after *Tickets, Please* and our script is filed away somewhere—but where?)

Next I went on loan to the Leland Hayward office to cast the new Irving Berlin musical, *Call Me Madam,* so I was at Hayward's every morning at nine-thirty, went to the Coronet, where the Hartmans were playing in the evenings, and went home after the performance to finish writing the play.

It was understood that I would be Bobby's first assistant on *Call Me Madam,* but the Korean War started and I was among the first drafted (my photo appeared in the New York *Daily News* over the caption "Korean Threat").

I got drafted (and it was exactly like being fired), but not before I had met Ruth Mitchell, Hayward's stage manager on *Mr. Roberts.* One day Ruth dropped by the office, a sensational-looking woman with a silly black poodle on a long leash. She was and remains very glamorous.

At that time I also met Lindsay and Crouse, two gentlemen of the theatre, who from then on became our friends, rooting for us—eventually investing with us—genuinely enjoying the way our lives were going. They were something.

I never got to work on *Madam.* I went to its opening night and I reported at 10 Church Street for induction, the reviews under my arm, the following morning at five-thirty.

I slept practically the whole two years, not just in bed but on my feet. I was stationed in Germany, assigned to an antiaircraft artillery battalion. Actually it was not such a bad time. Being thwarted in "progress" tranquilized me. I still think of those two years as real years. My life before and since hasn't been too heavy in the reality factor. When I left for the army, George Abbott said there would be a job waiting for me when I got back, but I refused to count on that—despite a stream of friendly and informative letters from Celia Linder, his secretary.

I was billeted near Stuttgart, and my evenings I spent in a place called Maxim's, a sleazy nightclub in the bombed-out ruins of a church. It was 1951 and in 1966 that club reappeared in *Cabaret*. Ultimately the years in Germany were to qualify as a business deduction.

I arrived after two years by troop ship to Hoboken on October 8, 1952, which happened to coincide with Abbott's opening a play called *In Any Language* with Uta Hagen and Walter Matthau. We were given passes for that evening and I went straight to the Cort Theatre in uniform, arriving fifteen minutes before curtain. I walked on the stage. George Abbott was sitting on a chaise in Raoul Pene du Bois' elegant Roman set, Bobby Griffith beside him. Abbott looked up and said, "Are you back already?" and I said, "It's been two years." And then, "When do you get out?" I said "Next week." And he said, "Well, come in next week. We're doing a show with Rosalind Russell based on *My Sister Eileen*."

My Sister Eileen became *Wonderful Town,* and during that first year of its success, Bobby and I hatched plans for one of our own.

CHAPTER 2

Bobby Griffith was producing a television show for the Ford Motor Company when he read in the *New York Times* the review of a book called 7½¢ about a strike in a pajama factory. He phoned me from rehearsals, suggested I read it, that he was too busy, and we might have to move quickly. I did and we did. By two o'clock we had made an offer to Harold Matson, the author's agent, for the musical rights. Subsequently, Leland Hayward tried to obtain them, and there were other similarly prestigious offers, but Harold Matson, displaying intuition for which he is highly respected, chose the fellows with the enthusiasm, if little else.

Abbott was not interested. He was not attracted to it: it seemed drab, and it was about a strike, and this country was in the throes of the witch-hunt. The notion of strikes, strike leaders, capital, and labor, and so on, all of that tossed around the stage for laughs when everybody was being pilloried by the McCarthy Committee seemed crazy. Still, Abbott agreed to direct it if we got it properly adapted. This, I'm convinced, purely out of affection for Bobby Griffith.

Every major writer of musical comedies in those days was asked, every major composer and lyricist; there's no point in naming them, *everyone,* and they all turned it down. Meantime, Abbott had been thinking and one day suggested that we send for the novelist, Richard Bissell, to see if he might be interested in collaborating with him.

Bissell was living in Dubuque, Iowa, a man with a business to care for and a wife and lots of kids. It took him four days to pack his belongings, pile his family into a station wagon, and move to Connecticut. Permanently.

Abbott's contract on that show and subsequent shows was more than fair. Naturally, he wrote his own contract, which was for a smaller percentage of the profits, a lower royalty, than the younger successful directors were getting. And there was no nonsense about billing size, position, no mandatory "boxes" surrounding his name.

We had no money, not for options, not for *stationery.* George Abbott provided everything. He gave us an office, the telephones, and we did our own secretarial work, and that's it. Although he must have kept a record of all of it, he never billed us. After *The Pajama Game* opened, we began contributing to the rent.

Frank Loesser introduced us to Dick Adler and Jerry Ross, who'd had a couple of hits on the pop list—"Rags to Riches" and something of Harry Belafonte's, the name of which escapes me. Adler and Ross wrote three audition pieces on spec—"Steam Heat" was one; the opening, "Racing with the Clock," another. The show was theirs.

The dancer, Joan McCracken, recommended Bob Fosse,

then her husband, an aspiring choreographer, for that assignment. There was no record of Fosse's work on film,
and we were afraid to count on him, so Jerry Robbins
agreed to back him up, if necessary, in return for co-
directing credit. Abbott unhesitatingly agreed. Robbins
was making the move which culminated in *Fiddler on the
Roof.*

Rosalind Russell, the star of *Wonderful Town,* introduced us to *her* husband, Frederick Brisson, who joined
us as a producer. The partnership lasted two more shows.

We capitalized *Pajama Game* at $250,000, and raised
our money the conventional way. We auditioned for backers in borrowed living rooms.

Freddie Brisson gave an audition early on, and George
Abbott told the story exactly as it was; in other words,
strikes and more strikes. In that one night we eliminated
every major theatrical investor in the country and were
forced to canvass people who didn't normally invest in
shows. All told, there were eleven auditions, which is not
really that many. I would tell of Romeo and Juliet in
Iowa, eliminating the strike, eliminating the pajama factory, Adler and Ross would play the score and sing, aug-
mented by four singers from *Wonderful Town,* and Bobby
and Freddie would "sell."

Edie Adams offered us her living room. We took two
bottles of Scotch there and some potato chips, and did so
well that we went back again. Twice.

In those days (and, incidentally, again today), there
was little money coming in from record companies.
Though Columbia eventually recorded the album, it did
so reluctantly.

When the show went into rehearsal, at the Winter Garden Theatre, we were still $28,000 short. The money we had raised was in escrow and could not be touched, so Abbott advanced us the $28,000, which Freddie raised to pay him back.

Bobby Griffith and I hired ourselves as stage managers. We needed the salaries. Until recently producers weren't paid a nickel until a show had recouped. They existed solely on an office expense of a couple of hundred dollars a week. Once a show paid off, they split the profits equally with the investors. But it took only fourteen weeks in 1954 to return the $169,000 which *The Pajama Game* cost. Today the figures are simply too high; it takes so much longer to recoup that producers receive a percentage, usually 1½ per cent, occasionally more, of the gross weekly receipts.

It took a year from purchasing the novel to opening the musical, which is not long.

In New Haven, Boston, and New York *The Pajama Game* was an instant success. Still we had no money. So on opening night in New York at the St. James Theatre, we saw our show from the wings while we worked it. We heard the applause. We shared the show-stoppers over the intercom system, "That went well, God, didn't that go well!" and so on. When the curtain came down, we crossed the stage and embraced each other.

I was getting $125 a week, and he was getting $250, and we'd go into Sardi's and someone would call, "Lend me a few hundred thousand, will you!" A month later Bobby Griffith saw *The Pajama Game* for the first time. It was six and a half months before I did. He quit stage managing it and I stayed on.

Going back a bit, we opened in New Haven and then

moved on to Boston. I think Boston is the best place to try a show out because the audiences are more sophisticated and enthusiastic about the stage. Business is good, if the show is. And the critics then were singularly helpful, discerning, intelligent. And fun to read.

It may come as a surprise that of two newspaper reviews for *Company* in Boston, one was a rave (Kevin Kelly) and another was a terrible pan (Elliot Norton). Still, with a very small advance, we picked up each week we were there and sold out the last. That's a theatre town.

I like to go to New Haven for similar reasons. And to Washington, D.C. What changes the Arena Theatre complex and the Kennedy Center have wrought in that town!

I haven't tried out in Philadelphia since the 1950s when the level of criticism was dangerous, encouraging audiences to support the wrong shows, not to be discerning. When *Fiorello!* played there, *Saratoga* did the business, and when *She Loves Me* was there, *Tovarich* sold out.

But it has changed; the *Zorba* National Company was interestingly reviewed and did business. Reviews of *Company*'s touring production were highly critical and unhappily accurate. More recently we opened *A Little Night Music* to a discerning response from audiences and critics.

The Pajama Game opened in New York on May 13, 1954, with an advance of only $40,000, which meant it could survive one week. On May 14 there was a line of four hundred people at nine A.M. waiting for the box office to open. And the following day we distributed a 20 per cent check with the reviews. We did this for some years with subsequent hits. But it was simply a trick. We deliberately overcapitalized our shows so that if we had a success we could mail a check the following morning. It seemed to our investors a profit distribution, and though they knew the difference, they went along happily with the feel of it. Our first shows were capitalized at $250,000, and cost under $170,000. Today, think what we would have to raise to insure an overage. In fact, costs have so spiraled that I occasionally undercapitalize (the figures appall me), running a personal risk every time I do a new show.

And I have never believed in the overcall provision.

It's just that I wouldn't want anybody coming back to *me* for more money, particularly when a show's in trouble, and, really, money rarely affects the outcome.

In William Goldman's book *The Season,* which is a survey of the Broadway season of 1967–68, he pointed out that I was the youngest producer in the theatre in 1954. With the exception of Kenneth Waissman and Maxine Fox (*Grease* and *Over Here*) and Stuart Ostrow (*1776!* and *Pippin*), at forty-six I am still one of the youngest—a dangerous state of affairs. He also suggested that though one of the most successful producers in the theatre, my only non-muscial success was Phoebe and Henry Ephron's light comedy, *Take Her, She's Mine.* Too true.

Some time after *The Pajama Game,* Bissell wrote a book which became a musical called *Say, Darling,* in which the boy producer, Sam Snow, was played by Bobby Morse, who looked exactly like me in those days. He still looks like me; it is I who don't. I was disturbed when Bissell wrote his book. I thought it was a cheap joke to characterize the boy producer as an amusing yes-man, a dilettante, who hung around "21" with a lot of beautiful babes. I couldn't get into "21" those days. I've never been a dilettante. Yes, I shaved at my desk. Yes, I paced the floor when I talked on the telephone. Yes, I was nervous, am nervous. Yes, it was even an amusing and sympathetic performance, but I couldn't see it at the time. I was too concerned with making a serious reputation, learning from Griffith and Abbott how to be good in this business because we had to be to do what we wanted in the theatre without interference, artistic interference. We had to put behind us forever the backers' audition, the patient and false consultations with the people with money about scripts and scores and casting. So any character imputations threatened me, perhaps irrationally.

I became a producer because fate took me there, and I was delighted. I used producing to become what I wanted to be, a director. (Ultimately, I hired myself, which is more than anyone else would do.) In those days to ameliorate my frustrations as an observer I would make a list pointing out everything that bothered me. Perhaps there would be 150 of them. Out of deference to the director, I would offer one or two or even five of them at a time when he wasn't preoccupied. Obviously half of 150 were taken care of before I got to mention them.

I learned how remiss directors are about going back to see their shows. Abbott does some, but not enough, and Jerry Robbins almost never goes back.

I always had it in the back of my mind to put in the director's contract that his royalties stopped if he didn't see his show at least once a month. But I imagine he wouldn't have signed that contract.

Years later, as an incipient director, I used to look in on *Fiddler on the Roof,* and though I knew I could help keep it fresh, I ran up against Jerry Robbins, who, unwilling to return to it himself, tied my hands, preferring that the stage manager keep it exactly as it was. Well, *exactly as it was* is not always fresh. Today, in my dual capacity, I can return and restage. I totally changed the last scene in *Cabaret* twice during its Broadway run. Perhaps because I had better ideas, perhaps the actors needed new moves, new readings. Obviously the stage manager is at a disadvantage; he cannot alter direction which has gone stale.

I have never dropped in unannounced to take notes on a show I directed. Such deceit implies mistrust of the actors. Instead, I give notice so that if someone is feeling ill, at least he'll call up the necessary reserves of adrenalin to give his best performance. That way I can see where the company has unintentionally gone wrong, embellished unwisely. Lost pace. I can see what really has become of the play, what values have been lost (or found!) and set it right.

Most important, I learned early when to say yes and when to say no and to base those "business" judgments on "artistic" criteria.

CHAPTER 3

A couple of weeks after *The Pajama Game* opened, Albert Taylor, an agent at William Morris, brought Douglas Wallop's novel *The Year the Yankees Lost the Pennant* to Abbott. It was, again, an implausible subject for a musical—baseball. Except for Ring Lardner's *You Know Me, Al,* baseball had been anathema on the stage.

Abbott read it, agreed to direct it, providing Brisson, Griffith, and Prince produced it. Taylor became associate producer. The score for *Damn Yankees* was written by Adler and Ross. Fosse was choreographer. This time Abbott shared authorship with Wallop.

We had no difficulty raising money then or for many years. One hundred and fifty-five people invested in *The Pajama Game* and in *Damn Yankees,* and many of them are still there twenty shows later. We never held another backers' audition (well, not as of 1974, anyway).

Even today a letter announcing a play, its author, the name of the composer, choreographer (often they are all new names) accomplishes the job. But it isn't as easy as it was the first seventeen years.

When we cast *Damn Yankees,* Mitzi Gaynor was offered the leading role first and turned it down. ZiZi Jeanmaire was in New York at the time and also turned us down. Gwen Verdon was in Paris. She was our third choice.

On *Yankees* a great deal of material was rewritten on the road. More than one-third of the score was jettisoned. All the ingredients for panic were there but Abbott worked calmly, and day by day everything improved except the ending.

When the show opened in New York, on opening night in fact, the plot called for Gwen, who'd been playing a beautiful witch, to be turned into an ugly hag at the curtain. The reviews for the show were good, but it came as something of a shock to us that the audience resented our turning the girl they'd fallen in love with into an old crone.

We went home with the reviews that night. We had a success, though how big a one we couldn't tell. At about six the next morning, I called Bobby Griffith to say the show was long and there were a number of things obviously wrong with it in New York that hadn't bothered us in Boston, specifically the ending. And how in hell, if he agreed with me, were we going to get George Abbott back into rehearsal? Bobby, too, had been tossing and turning all night and suggested we call Abbott at nine and ask for a meeting in the office. But by eight o'clock my phone rang and it was Abbott, and he'd been up all night, troubled by the length of the show and the final curtain.

So we met at Dinty Moore's for breakfast. We couldn't locate our stage manager, so Bobby, George, Adler and Ross, and I divided up the cast phone numbers and called a rehearsal for that afternoon, at which time a number was taken out of the show (we'd gotten away with that one in Boston, but *not* in New York), another number previously in the second act was placed in the first, and the end of the story altered. On its second night the show was twenty minutes shorter and stayed that way for a thousand performances.

We asked Walter Kerr back to rereview it and he liked it more than he had originally.

The only other lesson to be learned from that show was that despite the pretty good reviews there was resistance to the baseball theme. Our advertising had been keyed to a picture of Gwen in a baseball uniform. "Saucy" was the word. Still, we never sold more than $250 worth of tickets a day during the first four weeks of the run. So our success suddenly looked to be a disaster until we changed the ads to a picture of Gwen singing "Whatever Lola Wants" and excised all references to baseball, even changing the color of the ad from ballpark green to red. One Monday morning three and a half weeks later there was a long line waiting for the box office to open.

Bobby Clarke played the Devil in the National Company and he was miscast. We needed, or thought we did, a male star to tour. I had worshiped Bobby Clarke from early childhood and the possibility of doing a show with him was irresistible. Abbott expressed serious misgivings that we were casting a comic personality rather than an actor. He urged us to disregard the box office aspects and find a *believable* Devil.

Well, except for the absence of his painted-on eyeglasses, Bobby Clarke was Bobby Clarke, and though the tour was immensely successful, it was because of him rather than

Damn Yankees. Often the reviews said that there would be no show without him, that it wasn't much, but at least it served as a vehicle for him. Meanwhile the show had been playing in New York over a year and won all the awards.

Years later I was talking to Zero Mostel about *A Funny Thing Happened on the Way to the Forum,* and the authors objected on grounds that Zero was an actor and not a vaudevillean. Since we couldn't get the vaudevillean of their choice—Phil Silvers—they agreed, reluctantly, to go along with Zero. In *Forum* he played the slave. He was the actor. The story prevailed and I think the show was a greater success because of it. The same applied to Ray Walston in *Damn Yankees.*

It is not unusual for material to get short shrift, for otherwise good material to seem inferior, in the hands of a dazzling personality. Stars have a way of saving themselves at the cost of the material.

Not simply to put them down: I mean stars get to be stars generally because they're good, and if the best person for a role happens to be a star, then he should be cast.

But I think one of the best things about the theatre is that the star system doesn't really work. It's beginning to happen in movies, I think, to the artistic advantage of those movies.* We have always been able to do shows like *West Side Story,* like *Yankees* with Gwen, that create stars. There's no question that we sacrifice an element of security, the guarantee of a run if the reviews are poor.

On the other hand, it's an advantage I'd happily forgo in return for the star's creative demands. The presence of a

---

* I don't believe this about movies. I would give my right arm for Tracy, Colbert, Gable, and Lamarr in *Boom Town.*

star often perverts the material of a show so that you're giving somebody more to do than the part really requires.

And the star system and the whole business of giant advance sales boomerang almost invariably. What the public anticipates with excitement is generally disappointing. Now, why? Because to have a point of view about something makes it that much more difficult to be surprised by it, and the likelihood of its point of view being the same as the creators' is slim and not even a good idea.

Ballyhoo leads to disappointment. Most of the shows I've done have not had advance sales because they've not been based on particularly familiar material and they have not been star vehicles. So—no advance, but plenty of opportunity to surprise.

I've come to believe the astronomical advance is a precursor of disaster. Take a look at the shows that have gotten the biggest advances over the years: *Breakfast at Tiffany's, Mr. President, Jennie*. And *Dear World*. You can go on and on and on.

Very few shows open on the road in really good shape. But the ones that arrive in New York successfully are the ones that were polished, properly edited, rewritten, and handled well, and that depends very specifically on *professional* behavior in collaboration. So, if you find it, it's precious. Hang onto it.

Hang onto it, that is, until you sense that familiarity has dulled the stimulus of the collaboration.

Damn Yankees wasn't as good as *Pajama Game,* probably the next wouldn't have been any good.

Then Jerry Ross shockingly died, and the decision was out of our hands.

CHAPTER 4

After the first two shows we let a season pass. I don't think we were gun-shy. Nothing interested us. In 1956 we heard a score written by Bob Merrill for MGM, an updated version of Eugene O'Neill's *Anna Christie,* to star Doris Day. Doris Day indeed.

Someone had had the lunatic notion to take the story of a prostitute, written in the late 1920s, in a period of economic calamity, and move it up to 1955, leaving the rest intact. We offered to take it over for the stage, to backdate it, to help romanticize the story. It became *New Girl in Town.*

I've done two musicals involving prostitution: *Tenderloin* and *New Girl in Town,* and the subject is not romantic and rarely comical and our materials were too conventional, our vision superficial.

Ultimately *New Girl in Town* succeeded at the box office, but not on the stage, because the principal reason for doing it was that we hadn't done anything for over a year and were dying to work. We sneaked through with a hit and there is little pleasure in that.

A lot of musicals are created for no better reason, and often they work. But they have never worked for me. I'm stuck with "why am I doing it." And in fact, all plays that I see suffer the same criterion. I did not enjoy *Mame*. Why did they bother? I see that it's amusing, and I appreciate the polish, the talent involved. But the why anyone bothered, the *why* consistently gets in the way.

That doesn't imply that all musicals need be trenchant. God knows, *A Funny Thing* wasn't, but it had classical antecedents and it was conceptualized.

MGM was eager to unburden their *Anna Christie* onto us, to let us try to solve their problems. But first we had to see O'Neill's widow, Carlotta Monterey. Abbott paid the visit. She was charmed by him. We negotiated the rights easily and for reasonable terms. We then acquired the score, of which we were able to use only half because the contemporary material was useless in the new scheme of things.

I thought Gwen would be good for the lead. I remember George Abbott was somewhat resistant. She was a dancing star and it bothered him. But Gwen wanted to play it desperately and she was right to want it. It would show off aspects of her acting which she'd never shown before. It would stretch her.

We had heard Thelma Ritter was scheduled to play the Marie Dressler role in the MGM version. A wonderful idea, so we took it.

The best thing about that musical was the meeting of those two ladies in a bar. It was the best scene and it contained no music, which was symptomatic of what was to be wrong throughout the musical.

Very sensibly we set up guidelines to avoid traps. George had been reluctant to cast Gwen, not because she couldn't play the role without dancing, but how would audiences feel if they went to a musical *Anna Christie* starring Gwen Verdon and she didn't dance? And Anna mustn't dance. We all agreed with that—Bobby Fosse and Gwen, all of us, agreed with that. No matter what, this woebegone, negative, misanthropic wharf rat must not be choreographed.

All well and good *until* you get into a bit of trouble, and reach for the crutch. We're a little boring in there. *Gwen, put on your dancing shoes.* Which is exactly what happened. And the more dancing we added for Gwen, the more we hurt the show. *New Girl* was far better in rehearsal, when we stuck with a concept, conscious of risking the wrath of our audience.

George Abbott has never been a man to set someone dancing without motivation. In this respect The Abbott Touch has been consistently misunderstood. Dancing characters dance, doors are slammed *only* when characters out of emotion would slam them, and there is no such thing as a funny reading of a line.

There is a kind of deliciously unmotivated musical, a cherished memory of yesteryear, which some of our critics lament the loss of. Not I. I think that shows in which songs are utterly unmotivated, in which characters react inconsistently for laughs, mindless and pleasantly entertaining though they may be, through overpraise dangerously inhibit the future of the musical theatre. I think *Hello Dolly!* is one of those shows.

I think that *The Matchmaker* is brilliant source material for a musical. I think also that show was blissfully conceived, that it moved brilliantly. I don't think anybody in the world could have done it as well as Gower Champion, and I don't think it's *The Matchmaker*. I believe I would have preferred *The Matchmaker* because there are tensions in that play and because there are people. Carol Channing is an artist. She has powerful style and you can relax and let her take care of you. She also makes you smile, inside and out, but she isn't Dolly Gallagher Levi, not Thornton Wilder's Dolly Gallagher Levi. She can play this musical called *Hello, Dolly!*.

Now, there are serious pitfalls in my preferences and they tend to take the fun out of an evening.

A beautiful example of a show which was mindless, and as far as I'm concerned worked marvelously, was *Bye Bye Birdie*. What a good time. What a really good show. But try to apply to its characters consistent human motivations, try to direct them in those terms. I know if that show had found its way into our office, and I'd loved the score as much as I ended up loving it on the stage, I would have destroyed it. If I'd been the director, I would have destroyed it, and if I'd been the producer, Abbott might have seriously damaged it because all of us fed on the kind of logic harmful to the spirit of *Bye Bye Birdie*(s).

Birdie is one of the few mindless musicals I love. *Guys and Dolls,* another, is one of the best musicals I have ever seen.

But give me *The King and I.*

For *Anna Christie* MGM initially wanted 2 per cent for the basic rights, but we fought that: 2 per cent is too high.

Though as much as 3 per cent has been paid for basic rights, and the Shaw Estate exacted enormous terms for *Pygmalion,* that doesn't alter my position. I would have turned down the Shaw Estate and looked elsewhere. I still would.

A play should be budgeted so that it can exist at 60 per cent capacity.

We held out in our negotiations with MGM and ultimately settled the rights for a total of 2 per cent to both the motion-picture studio and the O'Neill Estate. And though that show ran not quite thirteen months and generally well below capacity, it returned its investment and realized a substantial profit.

But what is *Anna Christie?* And what should it have been? *Anna Christie* is an opera, and that is all you can truthfully, faithfully make of it. An American opera. Probably it would not have run a year *had* it been an opera, but that, aesthetically, is what it should have been. The book tried valiantly to lighten relentlessly serious material.

As soon as we opened out of town we knew we were in deep trouble. The trouble was that we had done it. Something we couldn't turn to each other and say in New Haven. Instead we set out to make a *better* evening of it, to make a hit out of it, but, and this despite Abbott, the panic had set in and panic decreed that Gwen follow herself every two minutes in a new musical number, singing, dancing, turning increasingly the workhorse, bailing all of us out of a shared embarrassment. Mind you, she wanted the new material. She wanted new dances. She, too, had panicked. (In fact, no one girl in the company could handle Gwen's chores. Three understudies were assigned to cover the role simultaneously!)

The most important days in the birth of a musical are the day you decide to do it (and that's when we got into trouble with *New Girl in Town*) and the day *after* you open out of town. Few shows open in good shape. The amount of work you can accomplish is extraordinary. But not if you panic. The fellow who goes to bed right after the opening performance out of town wakes up fresh in the morning, moves slowly for a couple of days, and then says, "Now here's what we're going to do," that fellow collects his stability (because he's got to be exhausted, having been through the extended rehearsal period) and gathers objectivity. I learned that from Abbott.

And, too, Abbott listens to people. I learned from him that you should, in fact, listen to everybody. Of course, you're going to listen to a lot of fools, but listening doesn't mean acting. Turn off the fools. But when the same observation comes up over and over again, doesn't that suggest *perhaps* you're receiving good advice? Don't be stubborn: listen. You really aren't threatened. You won't act if it contradicts your better judgment.

Abbott's work, even when it fails, *never* gives you a feeling of uneasiness. It has foundation. You never sit in a theatre and think, "Oh, God, what's going to happen?" You know people are going to make entrances and exits like professionals. You are in good hands.

Gwen, meanwhile, got sick. She was sick from exhaustion, and sick from conflict. There was a dance which had been designed for a scene in a brothel; Abbott and the producers objected to it as pornographic, an artistic miss.

The movement possibly was lovely (Gwen and Bobby Fosse thought so). Erotic, yes. But it had been imposed on the play. We had entered a musical brothel, our prostitutes became dancers, our Anna Christie, Gwen Verdon. Now every line from the original play which survived the adaptation gave us trouble. Gwen got sick and all work stopped.

For the first time we were pulling at each other, Verdon and Fosse on the one side, Abbott, Griffith, and Prince on the other. It's impossible for an actress who is learning new lines, lyrics, rehearsing dances, following herself on stage scene after scene, to be objective enough to collaborate on the construction in such a crisis.

We reached a poor compromise. The ballet was out in favor of another version. Gwen got out of bed, and Bobby rechoreographed. The outcome was a pale imitation of the original. Still as out of place, but inoffensive. So much for compromise.

I have no regrets about *New Girl*. I think the lessons learned were worth the trouble and we were paid for them. *New Girl* remains for us unique in that respect: a hit which I must consider a failure.

I never worked with Bobby and Gwen again; at that time the troubles we shared became imagined betrayals. Panic divided us, and we took sides. What was wrong was that we had collaborated on the wrong project. It takes time to accept that.

Even though *New Girl* ran 439 performances, nobody came to see a "Brisson, Griffith, and Prince show" for as long as that partnership existed. Mostly the reviews assumed that George Abbott had produced them. And later when Bobby Griffith and I were sole partners, there wasn't a sense of a Griffith and Prince stamp either. We got our share of publicity, but neither of us was a television personality. We never gravitated toward that. Perhaps with *Cabaret,* because I had directed it, people were aware of my involvement as they had not been before. Add the phenomenal run of *Fiddler* to subsequent shows and I think some people do come to see a musical this office does, but, and this is as good a time as any to say it, Broadway is not the place to look for loyalty from the public, and sad as that is to the ego, it is one of the best things you can say about Broadway.

Every time Richard Rodgers goes to bat, with all the affection and gratitude that people feel for what he has achieved in the past, in a sense he is still going for the first time. There is nothing to parallel films, where you can make a good picture in 1953 and work the balance of your life *because* you made a good picture in 1953! Sounds ruthless, but it's good for the theatre. And for artists.

CHAPTER 5

New Girl was the last Brisson, Griffith, and Prince show.

Propinquity began us, and when *Wonderful Town* closed, Freddie Brisson moved back to California and the distance finished us. The effort of sharing decisions with a partner on the West Coast was time-consuming and seemed fraudulent on our part.

The partnership officially ended when we took over *West Side Story*.

West Side Story had been owned by Cheryl Crawford, in association with Roger Stevens. Stevens had financed the formative years of that project. When Miss Crawford bowed out, Stephen Sondheim brought us in. He and I had first met in the audience on the opening night of *South Pacific* in April of 1949. He was there with his mentor, Oscar Hammerstein II, and Mary Rodgers introduced us.

It's curious, that. Steve was a composer whose reputation had reached me all the way from Williams College, where he had written book, music, and lyrics for a show called

Climb High (which was the story of a young man with aspirations to produce on Broadway).

Steve reminds me that soon after we met I reasoned with him over a bacon, lettuce, and tomato sandwich in Walgreen's that we were the natural inheritors of the theatre we were entering. I've always been an optimist, Steve a pessimist. I never doubted the inevitability of his acclaim, but I will persist that his pessimism accounted for some of the delay in getting recognized.

Back to *West Side*. The most interesting part preceded our involvement. *West Side* was originally dreamed up in 1945 by Robbins and Laurents as a story about a Jewish girl and a Gentile boy on the streets of New York. Soon after, Leonard Bernstein joined them, and for a time Betty Comden and Adolph Green were to write the lyrics and Leland Hayward to produce. Sondheim didn't join them until years later. During the twelve years before Bobby and I became involved social conditions had changed in New York and Laurents altered his libretto to a conflict of Puerto Ricans and "whites" on the West Side of Manhattan.

That musical was brought to George Abbott to produce and he turned it down. It was then offered to us and, based on the script, we turned it down without hearing the score.

I never appreciated how artful Arthur Laurents' book was until the play went into rehearsal, how concise, how important, in particular, the language he was able to invent to remove it *just enough* from real street language so that it would be at one with Robbins' dances. We turned it down and Roger Stevens picked it up in conjunction with Cheryl Crawford, which brings us back to Boston and *New Girl in Town.*

We were going into our last tryout week there, Gwen Verdon was out of the show ill, rehearsals were stymied, and I was on the phone with Steve. It was three A.M., and I had documented our woes to the last detail. Eventually it occurred to me only politely to ask Steve how things were going with *West Side.* With six weeks left before scheduled rehearsals, Cheryl Crawford had called the whole thing off. I sympathized. What else could I do? I had my own problems.

I said good night, lay awake a few hours, then phoned him back and suggested Bobby and I fly to New York the following Sunday, meet with the creators, hear the score. (Bernstein was very proprietary about that score: no one was supposed to have heard it, though I knew every note of it via Steve.) If we were happy with each other that day, they would have to agree to leave us alone during the remaining week in Boston, during the New York previews: they would have to wait until after *New Girl* opened. They agreed.

We flew into New York, had a marvelous meeting with them. Sondheim and Bernstein played the score and soon I was singing along with them, and Bernstein would look up and say, "My God, he's so musical! A *musical* producer!" I simply grinned, stopped singing temporarily, forgot again, and got complimented again.

Putting *West Side* out of our minds, we flew back to Boston.

Parenthetically, in those days I stayed on the road the entire time. The New York office was run by Carl Fisher, our general manager, and I would sit in on most rehearsals. They do get boring, so you go for intermittent walks but you never know when you'll be needed, and you must be there every morning for conferences. Abbott likes daily conferences. It's important for a director not to isolate himself from his collaborators, and strangely, most of them tend to, to protect themselves. The musical is the most highly collaborative form there is.

It was difficult to come out from under Abbott's protective arm. On the other hand, he gave us his blessing easily. George Abbott is a secure man.

New Girl opened on May 14, 1957, and we met with Robbins, Bernstein, Laurents, and Sondheim at ten A.M. on May 15. And *West Side* was cast, financed, a theatre booked, and in rehearsal two weeks later than originally scheduled. This was only the first time that Steve Sondheim would come to my rescue and I to his, as we shall see later.

West Side was unique in that it was so incredibly prepared. Robbins is one of most prepared people I've ever known. The contrast between Robbins and Abbott is interesting. Robbins apprenticed to Abbott in his earlier days. The very first shows he choreographed Abbott directed, and so a lot of the respect, soundheadedness of Abbott's organization, lack of emotionalism, lack of patience with theatricality offstage—this sanity influenced Robbins, has influenced me, has influenced others. But Abbott is less apprehensive than Robbins about material and Abbott's shows are more often than not created on the road. He leaves a lot undecided until he sees a show in front of an audience. Consequently it is not uncommon for Abbott to throw out a third of the score and substantially rewrite the script. It's his mentality.

Robbins, on the other hand, would like the opening-night reviews in his hands before he goes into rehearsal. He is gun-shy. He hates to go into rehearsal. He's the fellow standing on the edge of a precipice; you, the producer, have to push him over (which naturally makes *you* responsible if the show fails!). But when he finally goes, of course, it's galvanic.

West Side opened in Washington, D.C., in better shape than any show I've ever seen, much less worked on. Seven weeks later it opened in New York, and it was substantially the same. Robbins kept busy on the road because he's predilected to fixing.

Laurents kept writing, but little of it got into the show. The dance for the number "Somewhere" simply didn't work, and Jerry eventually improved on it.

Robbins has been called a "method" director. Actually he likes to dabble in it. He did in *West Side* and later in *Fiddler*. During the rehearsal period of *West Side,* he related the cast thoroughly to their gangs. Half were Jets and half were Sharks. They traveled in packs away from the theatre. They were young and inexperienced and identification improved their acting. *West Side* had no chorus. Each gang member had a name and history. Each cut out newspaper accounts of gang rivalries; they covered the rear walls of the Winter Garden stage with them.

There was a character in the script called Anybody's, played by Lee Becker, who was rejected by both gangs, so the cast rejected her. She took her lunch hour alone.

There was only one major crisis on *West Side*. It followed a disastrous first run-through, perhaps three weeks into rehearsal. The show was slow, lugubrious, somewhat self-conscious, IMPORTANT. Too much introspection, no impulse, no energy.

Fear struck. Laurents and Robbins, who worked well together, not always calmly, but productively, discussed it and Jerry was persuaded to remove the method, discard the improvisational atmosphere, to resort to old-fashioned line readings. And the company snapped to so quickly that at the next run-through, less than a week later, the show was in good shape.

I am certain, however, that the earlier process gave the play its legs.

I feel some impulse to clarify the comment on Laurents and Robbins working together well, if not calmly.

Laurents is a nag, astute, perceptive, persistently pressuring, assaulting, sometimes brilliantly, and Robbins understands this. He is capable of causing similar abrasions in his relationship with actors. This is not uncommon among choreographer-directors. The whole relationship between dancer and choreographer contains powerful elements of sadomasochism.

That process doesn't work for me. I need to have fun in rehearsal. I need the laughter, no matter how emotional things get. I shy away from contention. Contrary to my peers, the show is not for me the most important thing in the world.

We gave a performance for the "gypsies" (an affectionate term given to dancers and singers in an earlier time, when living out of trunks was the mainstay of the commercial theatre), sans costumes, scenery, or orchestra. I have never heard such a reaction. To this day I tend to prefer these performances to the finished ones, probably because the audiences are sophisticated, predisposed in favor of friends in the cast, and unprepared. Certainly production values should and can enhance. The trouble is that so often they don't. I've never seen a show that was made a hit by its scenery or costumes (Oliver Messel's work for *House of Flowers* and Christian Berard's for *The Madwoman of Chaillot* were equally ravishing). However, I have seen shows that were seriously injured by the wrong production.

In the case of the gypsy run-through, what people are responding to is an evolutionary process, which, if you've handled your rehearsals properly, comes at the perfect time. Your first audience is ready and your actors are primed for a first audience. The good in a production takes stage center, and the flaws are excused; after all, there are how-so-many weeks to go, not to mention *the scenery, the costumes, and the orchestra.* I'm surprised so few productions use the gypsy run-through. Perhaps they are afraid they are not ready, but rehearsal schedules should be gauged so that you *are* ready the day before you leave for Boston or New Haven or Philadelphia. There's really no postponing it, and occasionally a New York audience can affirm something about your material that you won't feel confident about again until you return to New York.

A Funny Thing Happened on the Way to the Forum had a triumphant gypsy run-through. It opened a week later in New Haven and died. It died again (and worse) in Washington. A play designed for laughter played to silence for four weeks and all we had to keep the actors and creators going was the memory of the bare-stage run-through in New York. It sustained them.

Also the gypsy run-through gives you extra days while you're setting up the show out of town to fix things that clearly don't work in front of an audience.

Apropos the value of designing: I remember I didn't have much patience for the blue jeans Irene Sharaff "designed" for *West Side* at the cost of $75 a pair (today they would cost $200). I thought, How foolish to be wasting money when we can make a promotional arrangement with Levi Strauss to supply blue jeans free for program credit. So I instructed the wardrobe mistress in New York to replace them as they wore out with Levi's, not with costumes. A year later I looked at *West Side* and wondered, Why doesn't it look as beautiful as it used to? What's happened? What "happened" was that Sharaff's blue jeans were made of a special fabric, which was then dipped and dyed and beaten and dyed again and aged again, and so on, so our blue jeans were in forty subtly different shades of blue, vibrating, energetic, creating the *effect* of realism.

Digressing, there is a famous drop which Lem Ayers designed for the finale of *Kiss Me, Kate* and which to my eye was a construction of black and white diamonds. I thought it the most thrilling thing I'd ever seen. Subsequently, working with Lem on *Pajama Game,* I asked to see the sketches for *Kiss Me, Kate,* in particular the black-and-white one, which wasn't black and white at all. It was black and white and green and red and maroon, and there were other colors, controlled and interpolated to create the *effect* of black and white. Black and white would have died on that stage. The additional colors energized it.

Jean Rosenthal was lighting designer for *West Side Story*. It was the first time we had worked with *any* lighting designer.

Credit Jerry Robbins. Credit dance theatre, which depends more on lighting than scenery.

When I started with Abbott and until *West Side*, Bobby and the company electrician, George Gebhardt, lighted our shows. It was a matter of lights up for the scene, and lights down for the song. Lights up again after the song, with George Abbott shouting from the orchestra, "more light on those faces—this is a funny scene." And when the laughs didn't come, still more light. (There weren't lights powerful enough to get *those* laughs!)

To give you some idea of how unappreciated lighting design remains, our most prestigious designers receive a weekly royalty of $75.

Though *West Side* received unanimously favorable reviews in New York, they were unexciting. It was another musical, lurid, perhaps, lacking in heart, and of course, the dances were stunning. We sold out for only a few weeks. I went to the box office the morning after it opened and instead of the hundreds of people I expected, there were only three people waiting to buy tickets.

As a rule, critics do not predict art; they follow it.

More specifically, our drama critics did not understand the score. It is axiomatic that when a composer writes the score for his first show, though the show may be a success, the score is rarely recognized. Invariably he must wait for his second success for his first good reviews. In the case of

West Side, Bernstein was applauded, Sondheim wasn't even mentioned, Laurents' book was largely ignored.

Walter Kerr called *Cabaret,* the first success I directed, "a stunning musical, brilliantly conceived," but neglected to mention the director. I was paid back when I did *Zorba* —disproportionately perhaps—for all the years that I didn't get reviewed.

As for the reviews that costumes and scenery inspire, I think they are discouragingly undiscerning. Critics are impressed by certain reputations (and not others), usually reputations that come from outside: Leonard Bernstein's reputation, Burt Bacharach's reputation. Visiting royalty. They're not *not* of the theatre, but they're not working in the theatre regularly.

Barring total approval in a review, I covet controversy. I wish there were more critics. I wish they weren't "trendy."

Too often critics disregard the ambitions of a project, settling for limited horizons. I don't want them to admire something with pretentious aspirations. That would be absurd. But when they measure that which is attempting to achieve something and succeeds 70 per cent in achieving it, equally with something which is attempting nothing but to amuse in old-fashioned terms and achieves it 100 per cent, then they have performed irresponsibly. It is easier to document laughter, hilarity, than the stimulus of ideas. If a serious play is lucky enough to be controversial, to cause storm, then it may succeed. But why should that be mandatory? If a critic is intrigued by a serious play, he is obliged to write intriguingly. That takes writing talent.

The question of a critic's credentials is another thing.

One theatre critic is also a dance critic, why is he there? One critic was a newscaster, why is he there? I really don't know, and I don't even care. If he's there to review theatre, and he's intelligent and loves theatre, those constitute credentials as far as I'm concerned. On the other hand, he still must write well or speak well or, in the case of television, project well. I'm one of those people who thinks it is possible to review a show in fifty seconds. You can read quite a lot of words in fifty seconds, and you can transmit quite a lot of emotion in that time. TV critics need not be pundits; I'll save weekends for scholarly tomes. This morning, tonight, I simply want to know whether to go down to the box office and buy tickets. Immediately—yes, or no.

The subject of critics and criticism which commands so much space, doesn't deserve it. Nothing new has been said for thousands of years. Without critics, people wouldn't know what to see. Good reviews sell tickets.

Enough said.

West Side played about a year and a half on Broadway; then we made an error. We calculated we had run out of our audience, so in a last-ditch effort to keep going until the road tour started, we lowered prices and initiated a two-for-the-price-of-one policy. Immediately we sold out; we had run out of one audience and *into* another. Ticket prices were too high even then for a substantial segment of our audience which indeed is interested in going to the theatre. Our pricing then and now doesn't cover a wide enough range: I know there are cheap seats, but too few and rarely ever in the orchestra. Theatregoers don't want to climb stairs. I don't necessarily agree with them (I mean, the balcony *can* be fun), but what in hell is gained by our obstinately ignoring the realities! Put more popular-priced seats downstairs and you'll sell out. And a full-price empty seat is emptier than a half-price full one. The economics are simple enough: you must gross a certain amount to insure operating expenses and a fair profit to recoup your investment. It can be done by keeping a wider spectrum of prices. This way I believe we would do away with the two-for-one policy, which is seriously damaging the theatre.

Anyway, we pulled *West Side* out of New York perhaps six months too soon.

It was too late to change our plans and stay. We had to book theatres, advertise, sell subscriptions well in advance. It takes a peculiar talent to know when to close a show and this office is short on that talent. I'll save that until later.

Our road tour lasted less than a year. Business was very good on the West Coast, disappointing in Chicago. Chicago is generally disappointing with Broadway touring shows. It supports its local theatre. "Second City blues" I think accounts for some of it. That and the fact that the quality of touring productions had been inferior for so many years.

We came back to New York, and I persuaded Bernstein to conduct the overture reopening night, and the critics to rereview us, with the result that we received the reviews we should have gotten in the first place. This time around the book was special, Sondheim was credited, and the show had a place in history. Further, they implied they had felt that way about it the first time around. But they hadn't.

We played another six months. Ironically we would have played even longer had I not gotten into a dispute with the musicians' union. We were playing the Alvin then and it had booked a new musical. The Broadway, a bigger house, was available, and we could have moved, dropping prices and enlarging our audience. Probably the show would have run an extra six months. However, it was no longer a money-maker. It was alive, providing employment. From a producer's and investor's point of view, there were no more profits in store, perhaps even some small risk in the move.

We went to the musicians' union and explained that if we closed at the Alvin Theatre on Saturday, we would be able to open again on Wednesday or Thursday of the following week at the Broadway. We could not afford to pay the actors, musicians, or anybody else for the intervening days, and I asked for a concession. They turned me down. We produced statements substantiating our position. I suppose they figured that our ego was so great that we would keep that show running even at a loss. They were mistaken, and *West Side Story* closed. The musicians were out of work, and so for that matter were the stagehands and the actors and everybody else.

Unions, not just theatrical unions, seem to operate on the theory that to allow the exception is to weaken the whole structure of the contract with management. "Give them an inch and they'll take a mile." I know management provoked it, and I am a unionist myself, but conditions *do* change.

Unhappily, negotiations with the musicians have not changed (see *Candide,* page 209). I have my problems with the actors' union, as well. Long ago I ceased going to Actors' Equity for concessions. Occasionally I would present their Council with problems which I was naïve enough to believe we *shared*. I was invariably turned down.

In the old days we always gave everybody a raise the day a show returned its investment. We can't afford to do that any more because the union is too busy ruling that a chorus person carrying a tray is in fact playing a waiter and must be paid accordingly. Or that somebody leaping inches off the stage in a dance is risking life and limb and so is entitled to hazard pay. We sit down and argue strenuously these absurdities and ultimately it degenerates into my winning some points and losing others, and finally someone says to me, "Don't you understand, these rules are not made for YOU, they're made for the crooks we have to deal with?" and I can't help but think, Why, then, don't you make special rules for me?

Everyone considers *West Side* a classic, yet in that year 1957–58, it did not win any major awards.

West Side Story was never appreciated in those terms until it was made into a movie. For the stage version Jerry Robbins won a Tony as best choreographer. I think they would have had difficulty avoiding that! But the show lost out to *Music Man,* which ran years longer than *West Side Story.*

But awards are like that. They give them out and it is nice to collect them. Much nicer than watching the other fellow collect them. Nevertheless, it is wrong to think they are an accurate measure of achievement. They can be; they often are not. It seems to me equally wrong to make a big deal of refusing to accept them: that gives them the importance they're not supposed to have.

What awards are is publicity. They are good for the theatre industry, fleeting fun for the individual, and only occasionally good for the play. This has changed some since Alex Cohen took over the Tony Awards, which are watched by 44 million people.

As for the film, United Artists was the only interested buyer. They bought it for $315,000, which was very little in those days, plus a piece of the profits. But profit participation in films has always been a chancy business: don't count on any. *West Side Story* was the exception. Though the Broadway production recouped its costs, increments from the tour, stock and amateur rights, and the cast album provided some profit, the film as of today has been worth over $3 million to the production. And there will be more.

CHAPTER 6

Only one theatrical poster is missing from the walls in my outer office. I haven't had the guts to hang it.

After *West Side Story*, Bobby and I read and liked a straight play by Jess Gregg called *The Sea Shell*, later changing the title to *A Swim in the Sea*.

It was about incest in a fatherless Southern family. The principal role called for a strong lady star in her sixties, a Laurette Taylor type, perhaps Shirley Booth or Helen Hayes. So we sent it to the Misses Booth and Hayes, and they returned it. Simultaneously we sent it to the appropriate directors—Elia Kazan, Joshua Logan, Harold Clurman—and they too rejected it.

The point is, we were dealing with the play *appropriately,* attempting to make it into something which had been successful.

The rejections continued coming in until we had exhausted lists of third and fourth choices. Eager to see it through (we had started it, hadn't we?), we arranged to try it out in winter stock in Palm Beach at the Royal Poinciana Playhouse. We reasoned that the play, littered with compromise casting and direction, would shine through a faulty production, that we would be able to fix it, based on seeing it, and to interest the right people to reconsider and do it on Broadway.

We had entered a companionship with self-deception, not unique in the theatre but unprofessional and lazy.

In order to try out in Florida, there are certain requirements. The play must have few sets, preferably one, to be designed by the theatre's resident designer and executed by apprentices, a small cast (room for apprentice walk-ons, perhaps?) and laughs, but the essential requirement is a star. So we persuaded Peggy Wood, television's *I Remember Mama*, and (for the sophisticated Palm Beach audience), Noel Coward's star in several musicals and more recently *Blithe Spirit*.

Nevertheless, Miss Wood was miscast. She knew it. She agreed to play it only for the two Florida weeks. Then perhaps, if it were rewritten, but that was a long shot. Anyway, it was a chilly New York midwinter and Florida was warm and we couldn't get hurt.

Truly we couldn't get hurt—not financially. In return for a small stake in a future Broadway production, Palm Beach would pay rehearsal costs, cast salaries, and furnish the set (suitable for transport to Broadway), costumes, *and* elegant social and sociable full houses. How could we lose?

In addition to Miss Wood, we cast two relative newcomers, George Peppard and Inga Swenson, as the incestuous progeny.

Audrey Wood, Tennessee Williams' agent, recommended a young director named Elliot Silverstein. How do you choose a director whose work you've never seen? On a third person's recommendation? Subsequently, Silverstein directed the film *Cat Ballou*. We were not so fortunate.

A Swim in the Sea wasn't all that bad in Florida. Considering the compromises, the ten-day rehearsal period, the reviews were pretty good, but then, local newspapers are predisposed to encourage their local theatre. *No one gets hurt.*

The trouble is that when no one gets hurt, when you limit the chances you take, *indemnify* the production, you go lazy, the "sure thing" evaporates in the same atmosphere of self-deception.

But the reviews in Florida were nice, and it had been costless and painless—so we came to New York.

Peggy Wood wisely refused to come. So did George Peppard. Inga Swenson reasoned hers was the best role in the play and a fit debut, regardless of what became of the play. Probably she was right.

And Elliot Silverstein wanted to come. So he did.

We signed Fay Bainter, who expressed grave misgivings, to replace Miss Wood (we showed her the Florida reviews), shipped the economy set to New York, and raised $100,000.

Griffith and Prince up until now had had four sizable successes, so it was difficult, impossible perhaps, to conceive of failure.

At the start Bainter and Silverstein loathed each other.

To replace Peppard, who had been excellent, we compromised on a charming Tony Perkinsish fellow with modest talent and little experience.

At the least, our venture into eclecticism demanded a perfect cast, sensitive direction, a production, if it was to have a chance. We gave it nothing but $100,000 and an opening in Philadelphia.

The play didn't work. Reviews were awful. The first of two weeks I kept to my room in the Warwick Hotel, to my bed actually—Oblomov. At the end of that week, Bobby and I decided to leave the play in Philadelphia, more accurately, to leave Philadelphia and to leave the actors there to play out the final week.

For Inga Swenson it was particularly painful because it was to be her debut on Broadway and she was good. As it happens, it merely delayed her inevitable success in *110 in the Shade*. For Fay Bainter it was a reprieve. For Silverstein it was probably a disappointment. It would neither have hurt nor helped him if we had let it come into New York. For Jess Gregg, the playwright, it was a great disappointment because he was deceived into thinking that something badly produced was better than nothing. He was wrong, but what alternatives had he? Griffith and Prince had optioned it.

As for us, the minute we knew we were closing the show, it was easy to leave the hotel, indeed, a relief to have had a flop. Moreover, we deserved it. And it was painless. Pain is a play you love that closes, but pain is not a failure. Curiously, we felt baptized. A failure lent credence to the events of the past three years, gave us a feeling of continuity.

Inadvertently the disaster provided us with the means to further impress our investors. We returned 52 per cent of their money with a letter saying we had closed in Philadelphia, had chosen to return the remaining capital and deprive them of an opening night on Broadway.

Actually, investors should take failures in stride. What they shouldn't take in stride are insufficient profits from successes.

Incidentally, we gave the scenery to the University of Pennsylvania in exchange for carting it away. Another economy.

CHAPTER 7

Arthur Penn called, asking me whether I'd be interested in an idea for an original musical. Over lunch at the Coffee House Club he handed me a piece of paper on which he had written the name Fiorello LaGuardia. He had researched LaGuardia's private life as well as professional career. There were surprises. Half Italian, half Jewish, Fiorello was at once warmhearted, ruthless, sentimental, intransigent, musical, a distracted father to his family, an omnipresent father to millions, endlessly petty, and immensely generous, a human being of heroic size.

I had always been fascinated by the personal lives of Churchill and Roosevelt. And it was some surprise to find that Fiorello shared their paradoxical inability to cope with their private responsibilities while solving the problems of the masses by using precisely the same human criteria they should have been bringing home.

Bobby loved the idea and suggested Jerome Weidman, who had written *I Can Get It for You Wholesale,* as a possible librettist.

Weidman was interested. We met in Rowayton, Connecticut, at Bobby's house; Weidman, Penn, and I, Penn agreeing to guide the writing and ultimately direct the musical.

At this point we sought permission from Marie La-Guardia, Fiorello's widow. LaGuardia had died in 1947. Though interested, she was anxious to protect her husband's reputation and arranged a meeting with friends of hers and the late Mayor's at the LaGuardia home in River-dale.

We offered to outline roughly the course of the musical as soon as we knew it, but withheld editorial approval. Our intentions were honorable, but in order to make a good evening of it, we must illuminate the martinet in Fiorello, his ruthlessness in behalf of his principles, and so on.

It was also in our plans to tell Fiorello's personal story in terms of his two marriages. It was Penn's idea that in the first act our leading lady would play his first wife, the beautiful Thea, who died in childbirth in the 1920s.

In the second act, taking place years later, the same actress would play Marie, his secretary and assistant during the clubhouse era in New York politics. He would marry Marie at the final curtain. Questionable larger point: you always marry the same woman.

We proposed the outline to Mrs. LaGuardia and her friends, who agreed to think about it and let us know. The next morning she phoned and said go ahead. The immediacy of the reply was characteristic of Marie La-Guardia.

The first scene Weidman wrote was of a poker game

among wardheelers in a clubhouse and ran thirty minutes, every minute of it rich in ethnic Italian-American political history. Weidman then went on to write a second scene for the second act, using the same characters. They'd aged and the city was in the grips of Jimmy Walker's fraud and corruption. Encompassed in these two out-of-context scenes, Weidman had captured the tone, the peculiar vitality of the era, the style of our show.

It was time to interest a composer-lyricist. Bobby and I had recently seen a musical, *The Body Beautiful*, with an interesting score by a new song-writing team, Jerry Bock and Sheldon Harnick. Bock had written *Mr. Wonderful*, the previous year, for Sammy Davis.

I had known Sheldon Harnick as a composer and lyricist, particularly of special material. Tommy Valando, the music publisher, teamed them up. Subsequently, he did the same thing for Kander and Ebb.

On legal advisement, since we had yet to sign an agreement with the LaGuardia people, and fearing pressure from them that we come up with Richard Rodgers or Irving Berlin, we suggested Bock and Harnick write three songs on spec, omitting to tell them the idea of the show they were asked to work on. We gave them the clubhouse scenes, which were not clearly defined LaGuardia material. They agreed.

Meanwhile, I trimmed the clubhouse scene from thirty minutes to seven and Bock and Harnick musicalized most of Weidman's dialogue into "Politics and Poker."

Bobby and I liked it so much we decided not to wait for the additional songs, but to make it official, to tell them what the show they'd been working on for two weeks was about. Whereupon they wrote "On the Side of the An-gels," the opening number.

The key songs in a score are so often the first to be writ-ten. This was true of "Wilkommen" in *Cabaret,* of "Com-pany," of "Racing with the Clock" in *The Pajama Game.* Probably it's a very good idea, as they establish (or should) the ground rules for what is to follow. The tone, style, con-cept, and often the point of the evening. Oscar Hammer-stein said most musicals are made in the first five minutes.

Weidman wrote quickly. The material poured out of him with no evident difficulty. And from the first, Arthur Penn seemed disappointed. He wanted it deeper, psycho-logically deeper.

But Weidman wasn't writing Penn's *Fiorello!.* His, and Bobby's and mine, was a more nostalgic subject, a lament for a bygone manageable New York, for the loss of heroes, of the innocence of speakeasys and payoffs and gang wars. Penn wanted more; more internal conflict; deeper, more disturbed interpersonal relationships. He had had them in *The Miracle Worker* and *Two for the Seesaw,* and he wanted them in this, his first go at the musical form. I be-lieved then and still do that he wasn't leaving room for music and dance, and, further, that Fiorello was the wrong subject for such treatment.

It's not that there exist rules about such things, just a *feel* of what identifies a project, of when the surprise *is* a surprise and not a violation. Since that time I believe I have proven a predilection for what Walter Kerr calls the "dark musical." So it was in *particular* that we disagreed, not in *principle.*

We parted amicably, Penn retaining an author's inter-est, and we turned to George Abbott to direct.

Abbott hated the idea of Fiorello as subject for a musical. In fact, over the years Abbott disliked most of the ideas we had for musicals and said so. Fortunately, he has no difficulty changing his mind.

We arranged an audition for him of both numbers and he loved them and the Weidman scenes. Nevertheless, our plotting, particularly over the thirty years we planned to cover, seemed unmanageable. One morning he announced, "You know what's wrong with your plot, don't you?" What? "That business about one woman playing both wives—that won't work. I'll tell you what it should be. It should be—"

He was hooked. What he suggested was that we take the Marie LaGuardia character, introduce her as his secretary in 1914 and tell the story of both women concurrently. This would have meant that Marie, probably in her middle fifties in 1958, would have had to be in her middle eighties.

We presented the solution to her apprehensively. She laughed and agreed to it because she's that kind of a lady. She knew how old she was, and she knew the larger aims of the play. And if that was the way to make the story work, then that was all she cared about.

Weaving the two stories simultaneously made it possible to cover the history of our city from the sweatshops through World War I, Prohibition, the Seabury investigations, to World War II.

The Abbott collaboration, extending to co-authorship with Weidman, worked easily: Abbott would outline a scene, Weidman would go home and write fifty pages overnight, then Abbott would edit, rewrite, and structure the total.

The only actor who came to mind for Fiorello was Eli Wallach, and he wanted to do it. He wanted to sing. We worked with him. He has energy, he looks both Italian and Jewish, and while he doesn't look like Fiorello, he would have seemed to. Curiously enough, Wallach is thin and Fiorello for most of the period of our play was skinny. (Once we asked Marie LaGuardia whether there was anyone she wanted to play her husband and she replied wistfully, acknowledging the impracticality of it, "The only entertainer who ever really reminded me of Fiorello was Frank Sinatra.")

Unfortunately, Eli Wallach lacked the vocal range required by the score. He offered to study, but he never would have made our rehearsals in time. There were no other candidates. We decided to find someone unknown, someone who looked as we remembered Fiorello, someone whose anonymity might prove an advantage in recreating a familiar historical figure.

In the years since *Fiorello!* either Alan Arkin or Dustin Hoffman, both established actors, could play Fiorello brilliantly, but in the 1950s there was nobody we knew who looked remotely like him.

Judy Abbott, who was casting for us then, had seen Tom Bosley in an Off-Broadway play, at the Phoenix, I think. He did not look like the young Fiorello, but he was familiar to us. He was a young man, a little heavy, round and jowly—not really Fiorello—better than that: a caricature of Fiorello. He read for us countless times, so often in fact that each successive reading was a disappointment. This happens when an actor is obliged to reaudition for a role. Having little or no coaching from the director, the actor naturally surmises with each recall that he has been deficient in some particular, that the powers are looking for something additional, *different,* from him, and so he searches in desperation for a new approach and for every good reason he gets further and further from the true intuitive choices he made originally. Such was the case with Bosley. Nevertheless, we stopped auditioning him (in time!) and gave him the role.

Let's stay with the subject of audition procedures. They are assailable on every level—except, can you think of another way of casting?

Obviously if you have seen an actor in a variety of performances or in a role similar to the one you're casting, if you sense his potential, then you can forgo a reading. But it takes a staggering self-confidence on the part of the director to cast someone for something he hasn't seen him play, on talent alone. I have known George Abbott to do that and sometimes I put it down to impatience rather than self-confidence.

The unavoidable danger of auditions is that some actors, quick and brave and shallow (we once called them "radio actors") give you at a first reading all you're ever going to get.

Other actors, some of the best, can't.

Abbott, having seen Marlon Brando in *A Streetcar Named Desire,* wondered why his casting office hadn't brought Brando around for auditions. Griffith hauled out the files showing that Brando had auditioned for Abbott half a dozen times and had been rejected.

Then, too, in the sense that the director has something in his mind as yet uncommunicated to the author, it's

sometimes impossible for an actor to give a pertinent audition. I'm thinking of Joel Grey in *Cabaret*. Grey, "born
in a trunk," singing in clubs and hotels since childhood,
shared experience with the MC, recognized the gaucheries,
the hollow laughter, the courage and vulnerability of a
performer in a sputtering limelight. But our MC was
middle-aged and German and androgynous, and all of this
Grey (or whoever) had to convey with a few lines from an
opening monologue and nothing more.

No one could have auditioned specifically for that role.
Instead, Grey sang and danced American style, and I told
the authors I wanted him and to trust me. And they did.
They don't always, but I've never been more certain of
what I was asking, more willing to take full blame if it
failed.

Unique in my casting experiences involved the lead in
Take Her, She's Mine. We auditioned dozens of ingenues
without success. Rehearsals were scheduled in a few weeks,
and desperately Phoebe and Henry Ephron, the authors,
and I examined the same worn audition lists in search of
a surprise. One girl's name kept appearing and next to it
the words No Show. Apparently because of illness, she'd
had to cancel repeatedly. She became our *idée fixe*. We
persuaded her agent to coax her out of her sickbed and up
to our office. Reluctantly, Elizabeth Ashley appeared,
beautiful and pale, too ill to audition, and she left. Abbott
turned to us and said, "What do you think of that girl?
Don't we want her?"

So much for auditioning. The point is, why not? Given
the fallibility of the whole system, why in hell not? It
seems to depend on how desperate you are.

Fiorello! was a picaresque musical, creating special problems (see *Candide,* page 192). We needed newsfilm to bridge periods of time in which the personal story didn't move.

For example, Fiorello proposed to his first wife on the eve of his departure with the Expeditionary Forces in World War I. She withheld her decision, choosing to wait until he returned from the war. So nothing *moved* for them during the war. You can't exactly ignore a war, and we chose to span that time via newsfilm.

There was little film on Fiorello during that period, only ten seconds of him shutting his desk in the Congress and leaving for Europe, but I found stock footage from a silent feature about pilots in World War I, of a squadron standing proudly in front of its plane, one of whom I chose to identify as Fiorello. And then in the film *Wings* I found a shot of a pilot complete with goggles, machine-gunning to earth a German plane No one questioned that he wasn't Fiorello.

Oh, the blind faith of audiences! Have you ever noticed that when you see a play or a musical, nothing ever appears to go wrong? Actually, there are very few performances in the living theatre where something doesn't go wrong. A piece of scenery flies up or down mysteriously in the middle of a scene or an actor misses his entrance (unforgivable) and the audience takes it all on faith, motivating everything so it comes out all right.

We made a lot of changes in *Fiorello!* during its out-of-town tryout. New numbers were written, some of the best jettisoned. The relationship between Fiorello and his women became lugubrious and sentimental. Righting it cost us a beautiful number, "Where Do I Go from Here?" which Marie sang in the first act. It is not unusual for the potentially popular song in a score to end up in a trunk somewhere.

Perhaps the most effective song written on the road was "Little Tin Box." It came at eleven or thereabouts (when the curtain went up at eight thirty). We were somewhat mired in the sad period of Fiorello's life. He'd lost his first wife and child in childbirth, and politics was going against him, and to make it even jollier, we were in the Depression. Faced with all of that, Bock and Harnick wrote a second song for the wardheelers, a companion piece to "Politics and Poker." And it stopped the show cold. Hastily, Abbott and Weidman tied up the love story and Fiorello was on his way to City Hall.

I remember hearing about eleven-o'clock numbers all my life. Though I don't care much for formulas, I would settle for an eleven-o'clock show-stopper every time. Those don't even hurt operas.

The major flaw in *Fiorello!* was the inclusion of the subordinate story of the policeman and the flapper. Primarily they supplied comic relief, in the 1950s a necessary part of the design of a musical. Ado Annie and Will Parker in *Oklahoma!,* the Carol Haney–Eddie Foy parts in *The Pajama Game,* and in *Fiorello!,* Pat Stanley and Mark Dawson.

There must have been a way to construct *Fiorello!* without relying on the formula. Nevertheless, consider its accomplishments. First, by creating subordinate characters, Abbott was freed from the constraints of the historical characters. And the subplot accommodated dance where dance was difficult to find.

The character of the policeman represented Tammany Hall, synthesized corruption in the city, spanning along with Fiorello the entire period of the play. Life rarely provides similarly convenient relationships and he was an amusing villain, leavening a heavy second act.

How to achieve all this without him? I have yet to figure that out, but if we were doing *Fiorello!* again today, we would have to.

The reviews were ecstatic. All of them. And the show won every award you can win, including the Pulitzer Prize. But it ran only a couple of seasons and that well may have been my fault.

There'd been so much talk about the price of theatre tickets, in those days tickets were only $7 and people were beefing about that. The Broadway Theatre with a seating capacity of 1800 was available, and after one year at the smaller Broadhurst, we decided to move the show to the Broadway, lowering our prices to $5, $4, and $3.

We retained our original company, had won the Pulitzer Prize, and we spent substantially to advertise the new scale.

Astonishingly, we did not increase the number of tickets sold at the Broadhurst by one. We filled the same number of seats but at the lower price. You figure it out. I simply assume the price of tickets wasn't the problem in 1961 after all.

There is another reason for *Fiorello!*'s abortive run. In the spring of 1960 Actors' Equity and the League of New York Theatres—representing producers and theatre owners —entered into negotiations which dragged on for weeks. There had not been an actors' strike since the famous one in 1919 which spearheaded the formation of Actors' Equity.

Though I wasn't around in those days, I remember seeing photos of Marie Dressler fighting to wrest some measure of dignity from the oppressive clutches of the likes of George M. Cohan.

This wasn't the first threat of a strike early in the life of a show of ours. In 1954, weeks after *The Pajama Game* opened, a strike meeting was called at one A.M. in the basement of City Center. Though its co-producer, I attended because I was also its stage manager. The session was a responsive reading starring Ralph Bellamy. He would scream "Strike!" and the membership would scream back "Strike!" In other words, he received a referendum to take back to the negotiating table. When the meeting was over at five A.M., we emerged and the members of Equity formed a gantlet for me to walk through as they sang "Seven and a half cents doesn't mean a hell of a lot" and so on.

Well, there was something extra in the wind in the spring of 1960 and I don't think it was the existence of a particularly inequitable contract. (More likely, it was the absence of a serious play that season.)

In the old days Equity was composed of two unions, one representing actors and the other chorus members. In many instances they have entirely different interests. In 1955 the two disparate branches of the union were joined, giving chorus members a heavy edge in negotiations.

Negotiations, which had begun in a small room either at Equity or the League, as we approached the May 31 deadline were moved to more spacious quarters in the Manhattan and Astor Hotels. Fledgling lawyers representing both sides were replaced by the senior members of their law firms and the rhetoric flowered and we were increasingly subjected to bigger and better scenes. It is anticipated that the actors might rage and fulminate, particularly the ones who had been out of work for a stretch, but the producers matched them. The lawyers, however, were the stars, and when news teams from the television networks appeared in the hallways outside the negotiating room, we were doomed. Given the spotlight on the six- and eleven-o'clock news, they were reluctant to leave it. What followed was, in Equity terminology, a "lockout." It was in response to a plan of the actors to strike one show on Broadway at each performance. This way they would retain their employment and be paid out of the union strike fund for the performance missed. The producers, realizing that the public would stay away from such Russian roulette, replied: you close one, you close all. We were blacked out.

Broadway, which finds itself hard put to get space in national magazines, was suddenly on the covers of *Time* and *Life*. We were the object of television cameras for eight playing days, but also of pressure from the Restaurant Association, the Hotel Association, the Fifth Avenue Association, the Sixth Avenue Association, the Broadway Association, and so on, to get this strike settled because, after all, it was killing *them.*

Coming as the strike did in the beginning of the summer, it made people reassess their plans to vacation in New York. And while the strike lasted only eight days, thanks to the press, in the public's mind it started before it actually had and lasted well after it was settled. Also, the beginning of a strike gets the publicity, not the end of it. The cover of *Life* was a blacked-out Broadway; when the lights went on again, *Life* was elsewhere.

The strike killed the momentum on Broadway. The impetus which makes for "tough tickets" was wiped out, and when we reopened there was considerable confusion from people who had held tickets for those canceled performances. Many soured on Broadway for that season and chose to take refunds instead of exchanges. I believe the 1960 strike cost *Fiorello!* six months on Broadway.

I am reminded of another episode during the blackout. Bobby and I were having a drink at Sardi's while across the street members of the *Fiorello!* cast were picketing the Broadhurst. Bobby had had one too many and was feeling grim about the state of the theatre and lecturing me on how times had changed and what it used to be like when he toured the country with his wife, and how spoiled we all were, not just the kids on the picket lines, but all of us. And he dredged up his favorite maxim, that the only theatre is a hungry theatre. Impulsively, he left the bar, crossed the street to reason with them. I followed. He was standing on a chair provided by the box office, and the kids, carrying their inflammatory signs, had stopped pacing and were ringed around, hearing him out on the subject of forty years in theatre—drink and frustration rendering him incoherent, all except the emotions, which were clear enough. The kids paid him more than respectful attention. They adored him. And when he decided he had finished, having repeated himself over and over, he climbed down and I guided him back to Sardi's. Crossing the street I said, "Bobby, if you keep it up this way, you'll be dead in a year."

Commitment to the theatre is a wonderful thing, but it costs. We love working, and we are frustrated by those business elements which we must respect in order to keep working creatively. Union regulations frustrate us because we ask, and I think with some justification, How can you regulate creative activity? The trouble is that some amount of regulation is necessary, that artists are taken advantage of because they are artists, that entrepreneurs can be sons of bitches.

At the heart of it, I think, is an indictment, not of a particular union, but of contemporary unionism. In the old days a committee from management met with the designated union leadership and over a period of time and anguish, it was hoped, would emerge with a fair and viable contract, which would go to membership for ratification. The fight, painful and debilitating, would be fought behind closed doors by experts and when the doors were opened and recommendations made, there was some assurance that they would be accepted.

Today the situation has changed and you can spend weeks in negotiations, come to terms at five-thirty one morning, the union team returns to its membership, holding a fistful of hard-won concessions, only to be rejected.

The next thing that happens, because the negotiators have bargained realistically, is that additional days are required, wasted, juggling the contract so that it *looks* to the hot-headed membership that rejected it originally as though improvements had been made. Meantime, there is either a continuing strike or the aura of one hanging over the industry.

Because of all this, I felt in 1960 that we had established

a strike pattern and that it would be unavoidable in subsequent negotiations, and sure enough, the next time we sat down, it happened again. But the strike of 1964 lasted a Sunday and cost only a Sunday matinee performance.

I remained convinced that every three or four years, depending on the contract, there would be a strike and I was wrong. Ten years later, in 1970, Gerald Schoenfeld and Bernard Jacobs, representing the producers and theatre owners, were able to keep an untheatrical lid on the Equity negotiations, arriving at a contract well in advance of the deadline, limiting publicity in the papers to a notice of the ratification of that new contract. Unhappily, it took a gasping Broadway to accomplish this. (Again, in 1974, a contract was negotiated without a strike. I happen to believe it sounded the death knell of the road. Perhaps a strike would have been preferable.)

Nothing I have said about the 1960 strike is news to anyone in the industry. Nevertheless, in 1970, negotiations between the Off-Broadway management and Equity precipitated a strike similar to ours ten years earlier. It and the contract which emerged, in my opinion, crippled Off-Broadway for all time.

There is more I would like to say about negotiations in general with Equity, and it involves issues that are not economic ones. For example, I have heard a dancer suggest, in negotiations, our putting a clause in the contract that will "protect us from sitting around while the directors and choreographers do their thinking. Why don't they do their homework at night?" Very depressing indeed.

Another characteristic of labor negotiations is the acceptance of certain excessively sophisticated rules of the game, such as: there is no relationship between the negotiators' private behavior (in session) and public posture (before the membership). Another: all that transpires during the course of a negotiation is respected as secret. I am reminded that at the height of the blackout, with obduracy on both sides of the table and not much reason for convening, as the deadline for the strike approached, someone got the good idea to bring in Moss Hart, who was President of the Dramatists Guild, as an impartial negotiator. Many of the other theatrical unions were suddenly involved—stagehands, musicians—and one of them induced him to call a secret meeting at One Fifth Avenue, at which time the producers were persuaded to make their best offer, and it was summarily rejected by the union.

Hart left the meeting in despair and the strike began. Ten days later when the strike was settled, the accepted terms were those which had been offered before the strike behind the closed doors at One Fifth Avenue.

Years have passed—for all I know fifteen years is not enough time to violate the confidence of that session, but I choose to, not because I point the finger at one or another negotiating committee, but because I don't think the incident is unique.

In the course of a recent labor negotiation which resulted in a crippling strike—not in the theatrical industry—one of the two principal bargainers was drunk throughout negotiations. When I asked impatiently of friends in the press why they didn't report what they'd seen—that, for example, one critical session had to be canceled because a

negotiator couldn't be awakened from a drunken stupor—
I was informed that there were certain unwritten laws
which must be respected. Why the hell should they? I'd
like to know.

CHAPTER 8

We had such a good time doing *Fiorello!* that we could not bear splitting up after it opened—so we did *Tenderloin*.

A friend at Random House sent me the galleys of a novel about The Tenderloin, that section of New York City in the 1880s named by the vice barons for its juicy pickings. It dealt with the relationship between a hellfire-and-brimstone aging minister and a young, charming, and unscrupulous gutter rat. The period was pretty to look at, the source material all too predictably *musical*.

Unlike the previous projects, *Tenderloin* was a natural. Everyone saw a musical in it. Producers bid for it, investors fought to finance it.

Today I suppose I can imagine *Tenderloin* as a stepping-off place for a parable of contemporary morality, the young leading man utterly amoral, triumphing, a forerunner of J. Pierpont Finch in *How To Succeed in Business Without Really Trying*.

It would be a good idea to cushion a realistic statement about contemporary corruption in pretty times-gone-by, but we did not do that. We fictionalized the period, romanticized the events.

Years later *Cabaret* to its creators was a parable of the 1950s told in Berlin, 1924. To us, at least, it was a play about civil rights, the problem of blacks in America, about how it can happen here. Walter Kerr, who admired *Cabaret* and said so, accused us of deluding ourselves. Perhaps. But the point is, it was there for *us* while we were creating the show.

Tenderloin's score was a good one. The book never settled on a tone. We had as good an opening number as I have ever seen, as good as *Forum,* or the train scene in *The Music Man* or, for that matter, "Wilkommen," called "Little Old New York Is Plenty Good Enough for Me." It was sung by the panhandlers, the pimps, the fixers, who inhabited The Tenderloin.

The character of the minister bent on closing down the brothels, saloons, and gambling casinos (in other words, cutting out the fun) turned out to be not such an ideal character for a musical. Bobby and I did not help things by casting Maurice Evans in that role. Abbott preferred Hugh Griffith, who would have given us an eccentric, lunatic characterization, but Bobby and I insisted on the Shakespearean star because it was offbeat casting. Evidently we hadn't learned from the Bobby Clarke experience.

On this rare occasion we made the benefit ladies happy, and *Tenderloin* opened with an enormous advance sale. It was what the public wanted to see. Or *thought* it wanted to see.

The public rarely knows in advance what it wants to see.

Eventually it rejects what it anticipates and embraces what comes as a surprise.

Clearly we were the wrong producers for *Tenderloin*. The whole notion of wrong and right producers is in discard today, the personality of a producer's work, his identity, is missing, and it seems to me therein lies one of the sicknesses of Broadway.

We made the first mistake in choosing to adapt *Tenderloin* as a musical. And then we just went on making mistakes. We had reconvened the creative team so we could be together.

Then we picked Cecil Beaton to do the sets and costumes, and Beaton did a beautiful job, but for the wrong show. It was tasteful and chic. It should have been vulgar. Beaton had the idea that we should make up the girls in the brothel stylistically, with masses of black grotesque makeup. So we took some of the prettiest girls you ever saw in your life and made them ugly.

Seven months later we closed the books on *Tenderloin* only 25 per cent in the red. The enormous advance meliorated the loss.

We never again did a show because it would be popular.

We did, however, go back to work too soon. I may never learn that lesson.

CHAPTER 9

We hurried into the next, an adaptation of *A Call on Ku-prin,* a science-fiction adventure written by Maurice Edelman, a member of the House of Commons.

The plot dealt with Russia's efforts to put a man in space. Jerome Lawrence and Robert E. Lee, who had written *Inherit the Wind,* set to work adapting it. Donald Oenslager designed a series of extraordinarily realistic sets: the chess pavilion in Gorky Park, the roof of the American Embassy, a dacha in the Crimea, and so on.

We budgeted a prohibitive $150,000, for a cast of twenty-six and a backstage crew equal to that of a full-fledged musical.

We were in Israel opening *West Side Story* when the script arrived with a note from Abbott saying he liked it and that when we returned we could cast for a spring opening.

Spring openings for serious plays are notoriously dangerous. You can't gain momentum enough, opening in April or May, to get you through the summer. It's a good idea to open a straight play in the fall so that it can run the full season, in which time it ought to have paid off. Serious plays traditionally don't play as many continuous performances as comedies and musicals.

However, we were in a hurry. *Tenderloin* had closed and the best thing to do was go back to work immediately.

Henry Fonda was the natural choice for the leading role. Henry Fonda was not available. We signed Jeffrey Lynn.

The night of the first preview in Philadelphia, the Russians, upstaging us, sent their Sputnik into space.

We had lost a race with the headlines. All the mystery, the glamor of the story evaporated. By the end of two weeks in Philadelphia, even I had grown weary of reading about the Sputnik. Newspapers were a nickel then, and *Kuprin* was old news.

As for racing with the headlines, there is a good reason why topical theatre is rare today. The speed of communications is primarily responsible, and you are safer dealing in abstractions, in metaphors. Once again, the theatre needs language, imagery, imagination, to separate itself from the realism of the six-o'clock news.

This brings to mind apparently contradictory advice which I collected soon after *The Pajama Game* opened.

Joe Fields, an author of *Wonderful Town,* warned, "Don't get so successful you begin to *equate* yourself with success."

On the other hand, Lem Ayers said, "Don't let early success make you gun-shy. Keep going." He and Saint Subber, when very young, had co-produced *Kiss Me, Kate,* and the phenomenal success had paralyzed them for a number of seasons.

The *Times* review for *Kuprin* was excellent, yet we sold one ticket (not even a pair) between ten A.M., when the box office opened, and noon. The public wasn't interested.

Instead of closing at the end of that week, we played another week, losing $20,000. I have heard it argued that authors have a right to an audience and that the investor, if he is going to lose most of his money, won't mind losing all of it.

But Broadway cannot survive that way. (I keep reminding myself; I doubt I'll ever learn.)

CHAPTER 10

Bobby Griffith and I met James and William Goldman when we were doing *Tenderloin*. They tried to help some in the writing of it, but it was too late. Still, I acquired from Jim the script of a play he had written, *They Might Be Giants*. It was about a wealthy American with a Sherlock Holmes fixation, about his family, who sent him to a psychoanalyst to have him declared insane so they could get their hands on his money. A fascinating play, beautifully written, imaginatively constructed—THEATRE.

Early that season I had been exposed for the first time to the work of Joan Littlewood via her production of Brendan Behan's *The Hostage*. I was crazy about it. The sure, yet impulsive way she maneuvered currents of reality and fantasy compatibly in one play was something. And I admired how she cued in fragments of songs—the show had many—and how they erupted from rather than grew out of moments. They had the abrasive effect of attacking when you least expected, creating such life.

Sondheim and I talked about that play then and for

years, and a decade later the songs in *Company* were cued out of a conscious debt to *The Hostage*.

We were in Boston with *Tenderloin* when I read Jim Goldman's play. I promptly scrawled a note to Joan Little-wood on some Touraine Hotel stationery, saying something like, "You don't know me, but I do know you and this is a play I'm enclosing which I think is extraordinary." I mailed it to her in London and by the time we got back to New York, there was a reply. "You're right. I agree with you. Let's do it." And that was that. We scheduled rehearsals in June at the Theatre Royale Stratford, in the East End of London.

What made me take an American play about American people to an English director? I wanted to work with her. At the time I didn't know how much she relied on improvisation and how little on fixed material. She'd done the play I've just mentioned and *Fings Ain't What They Used To Be* and *A Taste of Honey,* and they were wonderful. But the Behan play was reported to have been less than one act long when she went into rehearsal and *A Taste of Honey* similarly a string of scenes, with no cohesive theatrical shape.

Fings was the first Lionel Bart musical, and together they improvised it in a kind of freewheeling style, a precursor perhaps of Tom O'Horgan's *Hair*. What was so marvelous about all that was a curious irreverence and sloppy excitement—nothing constipated there.

The trouble was Jim Goldman had written a play. A tight, carefully polished play. I've never seen what Joan Littlewood did with Shakespeare. I would be inclined to guess, not very much. She doesn't take to discipline. The Goldman play was the wrong one to send her.

Meantime, *Tenderloin* opened in New York and hobbled through the winter months, and *Kuprin* opened and closed. We had yet to meet Littlewood. Then, early in June, Bobby, who was playing golf with George Abbott, collapsed on the ninth hole at the Westchester Country Club and died the next morning.

Giants went into rehearsal in June as scheduled. There were too many things for me to do in New York, so instead of being in London for that period, I managed to get away three days before the scheduled London opening.

Jim Goldman greeted me apprehensively at the stage door and ushered me to a seat in the rear of the second balcony. Joan didn't like producers much.

Littlewood's image of producers was Billy Rose. She referred to me: ". . . when that Billy Rose gets here from New York . . . ," but Jim assured me it would change when she met me.

The rehearsal I watched was confusing. As I became oriented, I realized that the leading man's lines were being spoken by a woman. Odd. It is part of Littlewood's technique to switch the roles around to give the actors a sense not only of their roles but of the total experience of the play. A valuable exercise, no doubt, but we were three days from an opening.

Jim didn't seem perturbed when I expressed surprise. At the end of that rehearsal, he took me down to meet Joan Littlewood. It was immediately clear that they'd fallen in love—artistically. He was a playwright and her theatre, in the still bombed-out slums of East London, was run on a sound Bolshevik line. (Littlewood was the Chairman.) Together they constituted a phalanx I could not shake. I didn't even try. I was too late, so I backed away and let it all happen.

Not surprisingly, two days before the scheduled opening she asked for one more week's rehearsal. They had had almost two months.

I spoke with Avis Bunnage and Harry Corbett, the leads in the production and longtime Littlewood actors, and on their advice I forced the opening date. After all, it was the East End, and Littlewood had always done her best work after an opening. Our reviews down there wouldn't affect a subsequent move to the West End after she'd fixed the production. This was Littlewood's pattern, and unless I forced her to open on time, the exercises would continue. All of this had been borne out by previous productions of *The Hostage* and *Sparrers Can't Sing*.

That decision was my sole contribution as producer.

She didn't like it, but once it had been made, she pushed herself to be ready, which simply wasn't possible in the two remaining days. But I had discounted this opening as the equivalent of New Haven, so in that context I wasn't too apprehensive.

We opened with the predicted disaster, and Littlewood accepted full responsibility for it.

For her, however, this had not been the same as the previous Stratford openings. She had fashioned those plays, in a sense co-authored them. This one had come to her total. Goldman chooses his words carefully, directs his scenes with precision, even providing detailed stage directions. All of this she admired, but it was contrary to the best of her experience.

Instead of improvising chaos, she should have mounted his play.

Oh, What a Lovely War!, rough-hewn, abrasive, inspired as that was, came out different every performance. *Giants* could not afford to. She knew it only too late, and out of her upset at letting Jim Goldman down, she closed her theatre and fled to Nigeria. *Giants* was the last of the Theatre Royale productions for many years, the last of that acting company.

Returning late on the afternoon of the day we closed, I found her waiting for me in the lobby of the Savoy Hotel, wearing, as always, the tam-o'shanter and tartan skirt which were her uniform, clutching a string bag containing a head of cabbage, some apples, turnip greens, and a Georgian silver flask inscribed in memory of *Giants*. Little-wood and *Giants* had closed the most audacious English-speaking theatre company of the 1950s, and I had intro-duced them to each other. (Predictably, Littlewood came home and is working again in that theatre.)

Jim and I returned to New York and Goldman sug-gested I direct it. I agreed eagerly, but I knew there was something wrong with the play. The Littlewood produc-tion had so obscured what was *right* that I arranged a read-ing of it.

I sent it to George C. Scott and Colleen Dewhurst, who seemed perfect casting to me, offering them the leads. They accepted at once. There had never been any equivo-cation when it came to Jim's script.

About this time Mike Nichols asked me what my plans

were for *Giants*. Mike had yet to direct a play. It figured in his plans and he would love to start with *They Might Be Giants*.

Arrangements for the reading went forward. We rented a room at the Astor Hotel, assembled a cast including Scott and Dewhurst, and though they read well, I got no closer to what was wrong with the play.

The reason was I couldn't hear them. Instead, I kept hearing the performance I had seen in England. Those actors, their voices—I kept seeing *their* moves. I hadn't liked that production, still I couldn't shake it off. It was indelibly in my head.

A few years later I did *She Loves Me* and eight years after that I was asked to make a film of it. I was excited, and we cast it well with Jerry Orbach and Joan Hackett. The Hungarian government offered unheard-of cooperation, to the extent that they would restore sections of Budapest, restaurants, and hotels to what they'd been before the war. And once again I couldn't start fresh. I couldn't seem to move away from the original stage production. It became a game of trying to recall what we'd done before, remembering too much on the one hand and not enough on the other.

I've always been amazed at directors, the classical ones usually, who can reinterpret plays over and over again in a lifetime. I can't do that now. I would like to someday.

I certainly couldn't do it with *Giants*. Unhappily, I told Jim as much at the end of the reading in the Astor. True, I could hold forth for hours about Littlewood's mistakes, but given the chance, I couldn't take advantage of them.

And because I couldn't, reluctantly I relinquished the play.

Scott and Dewhurst picked it up, but subsequently dropped it. Kermit Bloomgarten optioned it for a time. It went that way from hand to hand, but it never got to Broadway.

I don't know what happened with Mike Nichols. Probably then it was too late. As for the others, I suspect in each instance they discovered something was wrong with it, and, like a brilliant puzzle, the solution for it was always out of reach.

Because of the London production, Bobby and I retained the motion-picture rights. In 1968 they were purchased by Universal for a film starring George C. Scott and Joanne Woodward, and directed by Anthony Harvey. There was no cash in front from our point of view, but we would participate once the film was made. It was, and we did, and since then we have recouped all the money we lost in 1961. Which is probably the only time in my life that will happen.

CHAPTER 11

For the first time in seven years the New York office was quiet. We had nothing on Broadway.

After *Kuprin* closed, I realized that, at least temporarily, the prospect of a next project did not excite Bobby. In truth, he took the closings worse than I. He seemed to have lost his resilience. He announced he wanted to slow down his activities, proposing I do some shows without him. The firm would continue, but he would function in an advisory capacity, retaining a minimal interest in shows that were "mine."

Today it is clear to me that it scared him how massively he had overreacted to the failure of those plays, and before it was too late he meant to put time in the areas of his life it had been so easy to neglect. That's a problem shared by everyone who has a string of luck in the theatre. Success generally comes early, though Bobby was in his late forties, and continues in stretches and has a way of disappearing just when you need it most—when, paradoxically, you'd most appreciate it and you have nothing to fall back on.

His announcement of intention to slow down came in conjunction with the script for a musical I had read by Burt Shevelove and Larry Gelbart, based on the farce plays of Plautus, and called *A Funny Thing Happened on the Way to the Forum*. Sondheim had written the score and Jerry Robbins was set to direct. David Merrick was to be the producer.

The authors were having trouble moving it. Perhaps Merrick was reluctant—I never knew. Anyway, if it was available, would Bobby and I be interested in doing it?

Bobby wasn't enthused. I was. They went about arranging a release from Merrick, and I sent the script to Phil Silvers, for whom it had been written.

Judy Abbott, our casting director, had meanwhile read a play of Phoebe and Henry Ephron's called *Age of Consent*. It was a light comedy loosely based on the Ephrons' life with their four daughters. Particularly it dealt with their eldest, Nora, and the inevitable pain a father feels handing his daughter over to another man. We optioned it.

At this point, Phil Silvers turned down *Forum*. All those togas didn't seem funny to him.

But then, a lot of people had trouble reading that script. Six months later, when we offered it to the American Theatre Society, a board made up of producers and theatre owners, for Theatre Guild subscription in Washington, they would not even accept it for consideration.

There was no urgency with *Forum*. Though still very much involved with it, Robbins wanted considerable rewrites, and characteristically was reluctant to set a specific rehearsal date. So we sent the script to Milton Berle, agreeing to settle for an easy summer.

Less than a week later Bobby collapsed. Tommy Valando drove me to Parkchester Hospital, where Bobby was resting easier. I returned to New York, to be awakened at six-thirty the following morning. I raced back, arriving an hour before he died.

It is still difficult to analyze my relationship with Bobby. A brother, maybe, and certainly, in the area of stage managing, a teacher, a patient one, for I was emotionally ill-suited to that job. But he covered for me during those years, and I got out and into producing before anybody caught on. A friend. We loved each other. Ironically, he helped me in very real ways to calm down, to enjoy my life, more, in fact, than he was able to enjoy his own. He was generous, the delight of the panhandlers in front of the Lambs Club.

Michael Stewart, the playwright, once referred to Bobby and me as "the nice one" and "the loud one." I was the loud one.

The only area in which he treated me unfairly involved my growing desire to be a director. It was the one thing in the world he didn't want me to be, and he didn't face it.

He was going to semiretire, but he wasn't going to open the door for me to direct. He had always said that he was going to direct, even before I knew him. But he hadn't. I do not believe that he would have been a particularly good director. It had become his curious, quiet failure, something which really didn't bother him—not until I became interested.

In 1960, after *Fiorello!* and before *Kuprin*, Roger Stevens asked me whether I would be interested in directing a musical version of *Juno and the Paycock,* providing the authors, Joe Stein and Marc Blitzstein, agreed.

I talked to Bobby, and he suggested that we should co-direct our own productions. He had a true and unerring sense of what was honest acting; I had a stronger sense of what was good material. He had a better facility for working, dealing with people. I had the edge on him with respect to taste and the physical aspects of a production, the scenery, costumes. We collaborated well, but when it came to direction, we could hardly have been co-directors. I postponed directing.

After Bobby died, Abbott told me that for the past year he had felt Bobby's and my partnership coming to an end. I tend to disagree, but I am sure that insofar as the issue of direction was involved, we were on some sort of collision course from which he would have had to back away. Given Bobby's age, and his desire to take things easier, I believe I could have pushed through what I wanted. After all, I was twenty years younger. On the other hand, it would have taken time, and his death in June settled it.

We buried Bobby, and I took his desk out of the eight-by-ten office, knowing that I could never take another partner. Instead, I restructured the office, making Ruth Mitchell an associate. Carl Fisher, who had been our general manager, took on that area of the business which had fascinated Bobby and bored the hell out of me, for which he too became a partner. Bobby had been more proprietary than I, constantly looking over their shoulders, often unnecessarily. I was to lay the responsibility on them and turn to directing.

I read somewhere that one of the reasons for my success

has been an ability to accept the failures. Not true. The truth is that Ruth and Carl, Annette and the rest have always been able to close ranks around me, cushion me, buffering the world outside.

Sycophancy?

It's not the same thing, because while they may be shielding me from the outside, they don't shield me from me.

I like give and take. I don't like being in a room by myself. I can't even think sitting down! Probably that is why I take to direction, and that's why my direction is invariably on my feet and on the spot. I don't prepare where the actors are going to move beforehand, and we don't sit around a table for days and talk. It wouldn't be fun, and I wouldn't know how.

And we have fun.

Bobby's death cast me out into a world I had easily avoided. I had seen Bobby from nine in the morning to eleven at night, six days a week (on Sundays he was his family's), since 1953, inadvertently to the exclusion of friends and business associates. All that changed.

I went to Europe and in Paris met the girl I was to marry a year later. I entered into an intensive period of psychoanalysis which lasted a couple of years. It wasn't so much that I had ceased to enjoy life beyond the theatre and the office, but a free-floating anxiety born of the events leading up to Bobby's death, the fear I saw created by two shows failing and bankruptcy in his personal life. I wanted to do something about it before it was too late.

I came back from Europe in August and went to work on the Ephron play, which Abbott had agreed to direct.

We set Art Carney and Phyllis Thaxter as the parents and a cast of young people, including Elizabeth Ashley.

There was nothing especially interesting during the course of producing that play. It opened in Boston to marvelous reviews and plenty of laughter. When we arrived in New York, we seemed to have left the laughs in Boston, not to mention the good reviews.

More specifically, *Take Her, She's Mine* played the Shubert in Boston, with a seating capacity of 1700. The size of the theatre made for a bigger, broader performance. That, plus the greater decibels of laughter, created a perfect relationship between the stage and the audience for the easy, good-natured superficiality of the material. In New York we played the Biltmore, seating 948. The actors were forced to modulate their performances. Laughter was cut by half, and the play begged for more serious scrutiny.

We worry too much about intimacy. A year later I refused to move *Forum* (the intimate musical) into a large theatre, only to see it thrive on the road in a theatre twice the size of the Alvin.

Reluctantly, I moved *Cabaret* from the Broadhurst (1153) to the Imperial (1452) to find I liked it better there, a distance removed from the audience.

And *Candide* looked better in the Broadway (900 seats) than it did in Brooklyn (180 seats).

Largely because of Art Carney's eminence in television, *Take Her, She's Mine* played almost a year, toured another season, and made a nice profit. It is the only play I have sold to the films before it opened. It had some grace and some charm, and it was what you'd call commercial, and I had a hit the first time out producing alone. Moreover, although Abbott had offered me free space again until I got on my feet, that hadn't been necessary. I could pay the rent.

Take Her, She's Mine could have been produced by anyone. A number of the shows that preceded it fit that category. Others, the best of them, the Abbott shows, had a texture which was his, but even he wasn't so much concerned with content as I was going to be.

CHAPTER 12

While we were working on *Tenderloin,* Steve Sondheim urged me to read the book of an original musical, *A Family Affair,* and subsequently arranged for me to hear the score. The music was John Kander's, and the book and lyrics were by James and William Goldman. It was a comedy about a middle-class Jewish wedding, from engagement to wedding march. The book was funny and the score superior. Though there were sufficient conflicts en route to the altar, there was also a certain predictability about them, and never a doubt where the show was going. For this reason I did not want to do it.

Andrew Siff, a lawyer, optioned it in 1962, financed it, assigned Word Baker, who had done brilliantly with *The Fantasticks,* to direct it and Shelley Berman, Morris Carnovsky, and Eileen Heckart to star. Berman was in his prime then, but was cast in a subordinate role, the uncle of the bride, unbalancing the project. His was the best material, most flamboyant characterization.

I had seen the same thing happen years earlier when Abbott starred Shirley Booth in *A Tree Grows in Brooklyn* in what should have been a featured role. She triumphed, at the expense of the play.

A Family Affair opened in Philadelphia to a set of terrible reviews and was on the verge of closing without moving to New York. A call went out from Siff's office and from agents representing the authors to Robbins, to Abbott, to Gower Champion, none of whom was available and/or interested. Failing with every musical director in New York, they invited me.

I visited the show in Philadelphia. It was a mess. The material that I liked so much on paper was impossible to see for the production that was imposed on it, a unit set that looked like a tiered wedding cake, with doughnut turntables that moved at a snail's pace, and a cyclorama of wedding lace in front of which they played the entire show.

Instead of a realistic old-fashioned musical with walls, and doors, and corners, they had gone chic with yards and yards of China silk and surrealistic costumes. It had a big chorus it didn't need. It was a disaster.

Still, I remembered the material and if you could simply put back on the stage what I'd read, in focus so we could see *it,* that alone would have to make an enormous difference.

We could not extend the stay out of town. They had no audience. They could not meet the expenses, and we would have to open in New York in two and a half weeks as scheduled.

I asked for a midnight meeting at the Warwick Hotel in the authors' rooms with the three stars, one of whom,

Eileen Heckart, urged closing the show in Philadelphia. I opened the meeting, acknowledging the obvious: I had never directed a musical, but I knew and admired the material. Further, I believed I could fix the show, at least make something respectable out of it, but there was no time left for collaboration. They would have to do exactly what I said, no questions asked. They took a vote. Heckart lost.

I worked with the authors the balance of that night, meeting the company at noon the next day. To establish confidence, turn the emotional tide of the company, we tackled the most cumbersome, least successful scene in the show, a passage-of-time sequence. Almost every musical in those days had such a section dominated by a real clock, or clock music from the orchestra pit, and people jostling each other in tempo in the streets, in department stores, or on the subway, simply to dramatize via mime and music that it was "later."

I had an idea and the Goldmans wrote it. It involved new dialogue for Shelley Berman, who instantly blew sky high, refusing to do it. I offered to return to New York, no hard feelings—after all, it was only an hour and a half away. He backed down. I put the scene on stage, the cast applauded, Berman came to the edge of the stage and apologized, and we were in business. In a week's time we substituted eighty new pages for the hundred and ten which comprised the book, and moved on to New York.

Once I had decided to stay in Philadelphia, I remember, I phoned Abbott for advice. He approved, asking one question: if everything wrong with the show were fixed, did I think it would be a hit? I replied no. He warned me to remember that. No doubt I would do good work, the improvements would be real, but I must be careful not to be seduced by the experience into wishful-thinking a success, because that would turn an otherwise marvelous experience into a disappointment. Well, I was seduced, and it was disappointing.

Walter Kerr, who was the *Herald Tribune* critic, liked us. Howard Taubman on the *Times* didn't. The balance of the reviews were mixed and the show ran five months.

I know now we could not have accomplished what we had in ten days were it not for Baker's initial direction. The performers knew who they were. There has to be that solid a foundation for you to be able to tumult it to the degree I did in such a short time without destroying it.

But Baker was married to the wrong material. He has a natural sense of fantasy, a light touch, but here he was working with a Jewish family comedy.

The scenery reflected his misconception. I lost my temper one night and started kicking it. More productively, I ordered the carpenter to paint out as many elements of the set as possible, to paint them black, so we couldn't see them. I would have preferred black velours drapes to that set—but then, I prefer black velours drapes to most sets.

I took billing on the show. Initially, I wasn't going to, but it seemed to me sheer cowardice to hide behind someone else's credit. Though the show was not a success, word got around that I had worked well, and *I* felt like a director, not to mention that, in an interview in the Sunday *New York Times,* preceding our opening, Shelley Berman called me "ruthless."

I needed that in 1962.

CHAPTER 13

We had scheduled *A Funny Thing Happened on the Way to the Forum* for the fall of 1961, but Jerry Robbins decided the material wasn't ready, and that he wasn't going to wait for it to be ready, which left us without a director. We did *Take Her, She's Mine* instead.

Meanwhile, I arranged for George Abbott to hear *Forum* in his office, Gelbart and Shevelove to read their book aloud, and Sondheim to play the score. Much of that material depended on physical activity, so it did not seem that funny, and they were nervous, and it was very long. We started at eleven A.M.; at about one o'clock they were still early in the second act, when Abbott rose, announced a luncheon appointment, thanked everyone, and left. That happened on a Friday.

It was in the spring, and Abbott had begun spending his weekends in the Catskills, where he has a home. Later in the day over the phone he called the show sophomoric. I told him he was mistaken, that he would live to regret that he hadn't done it. I asked whether I could send the script to him that day by special messenger (two and a half hours on the Short Line bus). Would he read it again as though he had never heard it before? And if on Monday he still said it was collegiate, that would be that.

He didn't wait until Monday. He phoned me that Saturday morning to say, "It is absolutely marvelous. I'll do it."

Abbott alone, in my experience, possesses the self-confidence to alter his opinion totally without getting involved with "losing face."

Since he was committed to *Take Her, She's Mine,* it took precedence and *A Funny Thing* would have to wait till the spring of 1962.

During all this, I was negotiating with Nat Lefkowitz of the William Morris Agency, representing Milton Berle. Berle's demands were impractical. He wanted the world financially, and though I wasn't going to give anybody the world financially, that wasn't seriously at issue. More important, he was asserting his opinion with respect to casting, choice of choreographer, scenic and costume designers, even theatre. Stars have been encouraged to attempt such unqualified impositions.

I began to get depressed about the show. Instantly we agreed to drop the negotiations, however, my depression evaporated. We were left without a star, but with a star role to fill.

The idea of interesting Zero Mostel was mine. I had seen him for years in clubs, and I loved his performance in *Rhinoceros.* In 1946 he had appeared in an Abbott-directed musical, *Beggar's Holiday.*

But he was an actor, and this had been written for a burlesque comic, a vaudevillean, for Silvers or Berle. We tried persuading the authors to accept Zero, but they refused. It got nasty. Meanwhile, it was December and we were aiming for a February rehearsal and a spring opening.

Tony Walton had designed the scenery and costumes. David Burns, John Carradine, and the rest of the company were signed.

I was in about $50,000, which I could ill afford to lose. I continued to negotiate with Mostel, while the authors, independent of me or Abbott, auditioned Red Buttons, among others, and enthusiastically. I warned them those auditions might make the newspapers and that there was a risk involved should Mostel hear about it. They did make the newspapers, but Mostel wisely ignored it and we made a deal.

At this point, the authors, invoking the Dramatists Guild contract which gave them approval of casting, threatened to withdraw the play rather than accept Zero.

That, too, happened on a Friday. Again Abbott backed me up completely, saying if Zero weren't accepted, we would miss our rehearsal dates, and we could count him out. I sweated out the weekend. On Monday the authors' representative called and informed me that reluctantly they would go ahead with Zero Mostel.

(Apropos the Dramatists Guild contract, if you lived up to the letter of your contracts with any of the affiliated theatrical guilds and unions, you would never get a show on!)

And Zero was brilliant.

We had a run-through in New York before we left for New Haven. It was triumphant.

In New Haven the reviews were temporized—good, but not great. Something was wrong, but it was difficult to say what.

Jack Cole choreographed what little there was too slowly, so he wasn't ready. We had to replace both the ingenue and the juvenile. (Wonder what would have happened had Joel Grey and Barbara Harris, whom I'd wanted originally, been cast?) That sort of thing, but nothing really alarming.

The audience kept telling us it didn't quite know what to expect.

Recall Oscar Hammerstein's words about the first five minutes of a show: ours opened with a charming ballad called "Love Is in the Air." Burns sang it. It was well staged and the audience seemed happy. Amend Hammerstein's dictum. It isn't enough to "grab them" in the first five minutes. You must also set the guidelines for the evening, and set the tone. What is it going to be about? Up until now, we'd thought *A Funny Thing* was about love being in the air, but of course it wasn't. The audience knew that instinctively *before we did*.

We moved on to Washington, opening with a benefit performance, an audience predominantly of government officials and Washington hostesses. A bad idea. They began to walk out on us soon after the curtain went up. By the bows we'd lost over 50 per cent of them. The reviews reflected it. Richard Coe, perhaps the most influential and respected of the critics, suggested closing it.

Subsequent audiences, numbering fewer than a couple of hundred people a night, had a hard time enjoying it. Laughter needs company; not to mention that we needed their laughter. Try fixing a farce with silence from the house. Amazingly, the actors, led by Mostel, played the show, and there was no morale problem. But we needed an opening.

Jerry Robbins was in California, winning an Academy Award for *West Side Story*. I reached him there and he agreed to come and help us for about ten days.

Though I knew how much we needed help, I paused before I called him. I didn't want to panic. It is difficult to distinguish between moving decisively and moving out of fear. If you know what to do, don't vacillate.

Theatre time is unnaturally brief. I mean, a week on the road is only thirty-two hours of rehearsal time.

Immediately Jerry polished numbers, in particular the second-act chase, which needed it. Primarily, he concentrated on the opening.

Prompted by Robbins, Steve wrote "Comedy Tonight." *That's* what the evening was about. Robbins staged it, but it didn't go into the show until we were in New York previewing, and the minute it did the show worked. From the opening bar of that number, we had the laughter back, and we never lost it.

It occurs to me that Robbins could not have accomplished what he did in those ten days had he not prepared himself a year earlier to direct the play. As for Abbott and Robbins, they couldn't have been more compatible.

We opened in New York on May 8, 1962. Most of the reviews were excellent (John Chapman of the *News* loathed it). We had an advance of only $40,000, and it was late in the season. Something about even the ecstatic reviews suggested ours wasn't a show for everyone. We worried for the next eight weeks with summer approaching. By the end of June we were selling out.

Sondheim had his first success as a composer, though his music was barely acknowledged, and when it was, invariably suffered by comparison with his lyrics.

Ultimately, it won the Tony Award as Best Musical of 1962, though Sondheim was not even nominated for writing the score.

In 1972 Burt Shevelove directed it (finally) with Phil Silvers. But Sondheim became the star of it, the same critics forgetting their initial reviews. And though the reviews were marvelous (better than they had been originally), I believe it wasn't nearly as good. Phil Silvers was the vaudevillean Mostel hadn't been, and the year became A.D. 1972, instead of 200 B.C.

I missed Walton's production, particularly the lighting scheme he and Richard Pilbrow designed for the show. To emphasize the dimensions of the set, they built two towers on either side of the stage from which they projected on a cyclorama upstage dozens of changing abstract images, one enhancing a love song, another emphasizing the midday madness of scenes, tranquilizing, exhilarating, keeping pace with the busy moods of the show.

Walton had to handpaint on glass slides, which were then distorted by Pilbrow in London so that as they were cast at an angle of forty-five degrees, the distortion compensated for the distance they covered. It was involved and expensive, and worth it. I didn't realize how worth it until we toured the show without them.

I hate to admit it, but the latest *Forum* rankled me, for another reason. There is a rule in the existing Dramatists

Guild contract that provides that four and a half months after a first-class production of a Broadway or touring play closes, the first-class rights revert to the authors.

A Funny Thing was a particularly difficult show to make a hit of. There is no way to separate the contributions of the director and producer from the success of that show, particularly in view of how much trouble it was out of town. It is impossible to say who suggests what and when. The point is that neither Abbott nor I, nor the hundred fifty-odd original investors, participated in the revival, which followed us by only ten years.

Surely there is a fair solution in a sliding scale which provides that the longer a show runs, the longer the original production participates. I resent that my heirs won't share in perpetuity in the success of *West Side Story*. As for *Fiddler*, though it ran almost eight years, a first-class production could be mounted tomorrow without our receiving a dime.

And if the quality of that production were poor, it might devalue the subsidiary rights, in which we do participate.

CHAPTER 14

Early in 1962, Bock and Harnick came to me with a completed *Tevye and His Daughters,* and I told them that unless they could get Jerome Robbins to direct it, they mustn't do it. Robbins was unavailable so they put it away.

They had another show ready, and it was *She Loves Me,* only then it was called *The Shop Around the Corner.* I agreed to co-produce it with Lawrence Kasha and Philip McKenna, who owned it.

I asked them to see a production of *The Matchmaker* I had directed for the Phoenix, which was touring New York State. They did, and asked me to direct *She Loves Me.* That was the idea.

Gower Champion had been interested in *The Shop Around the Corner* earlier and then had decided to do something else. The something else fell through while we were in the midst of rewriting *She Loves Me.* Gower became available and told them that he had reconsidered. I offered to step aside. How could I keep them from Champion, who had staged *Carnival* and *Bye Bye Birdie* by then?

They stayed with me, which loyalty I've always appreciated, because if Gower had done it, it might have been a big hit. But it wouldn't have been *She Loves Me.*

About the same time this was happening, David Merrick heard about *The Matchmaker* and asked me to do what was then called *Dolly! A Damned Exasperating Woman.* I turned it down. Among other reasons, I didn't care for the score, particularly the song "Hello, Dolly!" I couldn't for the life of me see why those waiters were singing how glad they were to have her back where she belonged, when she'd never been there in the first place.

If you look at the basic material of *The Matchmaker* and *The Shop Around the Corner,* you can see certain obvious similarities. The Harmonia Gardens and the Café Imperiale in *She Loves Me* are the same place. Mistaken identity figures in both plots. The love relationships are naïve, awkward.

She Loves Me is one of the best things this office has done, and as far as I'm concerned, it's as well directed as anything I've ever done.

If you want to analyze carefully why it ran only nine and one half months on Broadway, and as of this writing has never been made into a movie, I have given it more thought than I like to give projects after the fact.

It was a style piece, an unsentimental love story. It had irony and an edge to it. It was funny, but not hilarious. It was melodic, but not soaring. There were only two dances, and they were small. No one came to the edge of the footlights and gave it to you. It was soft-sell.

And in 1963, we were at the peak of the noisy heavy-sell musical.

Joe Masteroff wrote a beautiful book, Jerry Bock and Sheldon Harnick a near-perfect score. It was orchestrated for strings. The cast included Barbara Cook, Barbara Baxley, Dan Massey, Jack Cassidy. It was a company of actors, expert actors.

I may be making more of *She Loves Me* than I should. It was my first solo directing-from-scratch assignment. It received six excellent reviews from the dailies. Only Walter Kerr, writing for the *Herald Tribune,* disliked it. He likes his musicals to punch, and this didn't. But the good reviews were unexciting. It was a "dear" show, long on sentiment, charm, nostalgia (bad word *then:* what if we had opened in 1974?), a valentine.

We knew in a few weeks that it would never make it. Generally you can. The trouble is facing it. There are those exceptions, *Abie's Irish Rose, Wish You Were Here,* to keep you hoping. But they are exceptions, and almost always the trajectory of a show's popularity is a descending curve. Eventually we lost most of the $300,000 investment, but it took nine long suffering months.

Originally, Julie Andrews wanted to play the lead. She was filming *The Americanization of Emily* and requested we wait six months for her. I didn't. I was in a hurry to work. Good as Barbara Cook was in *She Loves Me,* Julie Andrews would have overridden the sugary reviews. Had I waited six months, the show might have run three years.

I had difficulties with actors on this show, the difficulties I would have had on *A Family Affair* had those actors not been so desperate for help. I am trusted now. I can be as scared on the first day of rehearsal as I was then, but it is different. My record gives them the confidence they need. Actors test directors, much as children do parents, to see how far they can go (often they don't know where they want to go), to see how protected they are.

Today I can go dry, waste a day working in the wrong direction. All I have to do is admit it. Invariably it works to my advantage, giving the relationship the mutuality rehearsing requires.

In 1963 I didn't know that. I knew only to stay strong and to keep my perspective of the total. The good director sees the whole play. Many people can direct good scenes. The problem is directing good plays. Abbott and Robbins know from beginning to end what the evening is going to be. They may not know details along the way, but they see the total.

Carol Haney choreographed *She Loves Me*. We'd been friends since *The Pajama Game,* and she had a witty and imaginative mind and a collaborator's desire for the total. She was modest about her work. It's a modest show, the stars, the director, the choreographer, nobody "took stage," nobody showed off. Unhappily, neither did the critics.

It opened late in April and ran until February the following year, meeting expenses, occasionally showing a small profit, all the while going gradually downhill. I should have closed it at the end of December. Had I, we would have returned $60,000 to the investors. Instead, I threw that sum away on an additional three weeks. All for the love of a show.

She Loves Me played the 1046-seat Eugene O'Neill Theatre. Aesthetically, the ideal theatre, but to meet our expenses, totally impractical. There's a theory in this business that there are either hits or flops. It isn't true. Of the seventeen musicals I've produced, only five played to capacity for any length of time. In the case of *She Loves Me* (as in *Take Her, She's Mine*), I overestimated the importance of the size of the theatre on the play's effectiveness.

There's no question but that there is a kind of play that needs an intimate theatre, but that intimacy exists only Off-Broadway or in the Booth Theatre and is common to England and the Continent. Excepting the D. H. Lawrence plays at the Royal Court, I know of nothing that could not be transferred painlessly from a six hundred seat house to a twelve hundred seat house.

She Loves Me played wonderfully in the O'Neill, but it would have played equally well in a theatre half again as large, and we would have made up on Wednesday and Saturday matinees, on Friday and Saturday nights, what we lost on Mondays and Tuesdays, and doubled our run on Broadway.

In that extra year I know we would have sold it to the movies and probably repaid the investment. Julie Andrews and Dick Van Dyke wanted to make a film of it. They had just finished *Mary Poppins* for Disney, but it had not been released and in the additional time *Mary Poppins* would have become the success it did, they would have had their way, and we would have sold our musical.

Until recently I tended to think of *She Loves Me* as a flop—because it lost money. But a work is not necessarily measured in its own time properly. Success is not measured at the box office. The chances are, if you work often enough, consistently enough, some of your best work will be underestimated, some of your poorer work will get by. If you work consistently enough, it balances out. But in 1963 there was no doubt about it: *She Loves Me* was a flop. I could not continue losing my investors' money. The next one would have to be a hit. Not just a good show, a hit. The Robbins–Abbott shows made a profit.

As for the good reviews *She Loves Me* received, I wasn't mentioned in them. Presumably it had directed itself. So if I wanted to continue directing on Broadway, not only did I have to return the investment, I would have to get reviewed.

It has been said that in the best direction you do not see the director's hand. That isn't necessarily true. Brecht was hardly unobtrusive. I was always aware of Kazan. There are projects that should not be "co-authored" by the director, but I felt I must find a project that begged for such authority my next time out.

However, I wasn't ready to grapple with that yet. Instead, I went back to familiar territory, to Robbins and to *Fiddler on the Roof*.

CHAPTER 15

When I first read *Fiddler* in 1962, it was fascinating, but alien. My background is German-Jewish—different from Russian-Jewish. Joe Stein gave me the script, then called *Tevye,* and Bock and Harnick a book, *Life Is with People,* a sociological examination of communal life created by the Jews forced to live separately in shtetls.

The original script was realistic. It opened with Tevye and his family at Sabbath prayers, concerned less with the community and still less with the larger world outside. It lacked size.

I thought it primarily ethnic, and in that sense special. Great art transcends particular milieus. Marc Chagall, using the same shtetl, creates universal art. I reckoned Robbins would do the same. Unfortunately, at the time, Robbins was working on *Funny Girl* and was unavailable.

Bock and Harnick and I did *She Loves Me* instead.

A year later Fred Coe optioned *Tevye.* By then, Robbins had dropped *Funny Girl* and accepted *Tevye* on the condition that I be brought in as a co-producer. *She Loves*

Me was floundering, so I jumped, providing that my office produce the show.

Fred Coe was directing his first film, *A Thousand Clowns,* and seemed happy to relinquish the burden.

Robbins set about giving *Tevye* its size. In a larger sense, what was the musical about? Or rather, what should it be about? The struggle of parents to preserve traditions against the pressures of changing times. Robbins began restructuring the story, postponing the introduction of Tevye's family at Sabbath prayers, opening instead with the community, the whole company in a number, sung and danced (stylization created size), entitled "Tradition."

Once this was established, the townspeople, including Tevye and his family, became individuals. In the case of *Fiddler,* each member of the company had a story, a vocation, a life.

There wasn't much dancing in *Fiddler,* excepting for the opening number and one in the second act for Tevye's wife and three daughters (it grew out of second-act problems and was expedient). Robbins wanted the dances to be naturalistic, informal, as they would have been in a tavern, at a wedding celebration.

The point was to separate sharply realism (the events) from the poetically abstract (the message).

I suppose no man is indispensable, but on *Fiddler* I think Robbins was.

Tom Bosley was Jerry's choice for Tevye, not mine. I opted for a presence, specifically, Zero Mostel's. I was still worrying that there might be resistance and wanted creative and economic insurance. It was expensive. Zero refused to sign for more than nine months. The short-term contract appealed to me because in an interesting way it gave me the advantage in our relationship. I knew Zero. After a play has opened, he tends to get bored, amuses himself on stage to keep things interesting. He refused to take notes from anyone for the run of his *Forum* contract, and that show quickly lost the element in his performance which made it extraordinary—the character of the slave. Ironically, the actor had abdicated to the performer, pursuing laughs and ingenious bits of business, obliterating the story.

More generally, if an actor is signed to a long-term contract in a starring role and becomes identified with the show, it's very possible and even likely he will be encouraged to make greater and greater demands on the management because he feels indispensable.

On the other hand, if the actor is on a short-term contract, he may reason that when the show is a smash, he can renegotiate an extension and do even better. Zero's lawyer had just that in mind. After nine months of hearing it called the Zero Mostel musical and considerable pressure from the theatre owners to resign Zero on any basis, we decided to rely on the material.

At this point, all other terms had been negotiated, and we were arguing about providing a car and a chauffeur for the star to and from the theatre. I turned them down. And the show reverted to Tevye and his daughters.

I still think Zero was the best in the role when he was at his best, but had he left after three years instead of nine months, undoubtedly it would have cut down on our run.

Robbins chose Boris Aronson to design the scenery. I consider the day I met Boris second only to the day I met

Abbott. Yet *Fiddler* did not tap the best of Aronson. He recently told me that if he had *Fiddler* to design again, he would do it differently because it was too influenced by Chagall, which was what Jerry wanted at the time.

Subsequently, his designs for *Cabaret, Zorba, Company, Follies,* and even *Night Music,* expressed him as *Fiddler* did not. Over the years Boris and I, mutually encouraging, moved further and further from naturalism, from props and doors and tables, and units, wagons with rooms on them, until with *Follies* there were no tables, no chairs, no doors, no windows.

Pat Zipprodt, straight from *She Loves Me,* designed the most expensive rags for the company to wear. It was *West Side Story* again. The colors of the peasants' clothes were beautifully controlled, then beaten and aged in a vat of dye, then shown to Jerry, who would say take them back and age them, and they would be beaten some more and dipped in dye and returned for his approval, which came reluctantly.

Everything was expensive on that show, but not for the usual reasons. Robbins, directing and choreographing, insisted on eight weeks' rehearsal. The "chorus," middle-aged, cast to type, required considerable acting experience, representing a high weekly operating expense. In 1964 the payroll for the cast, including Zero, was $15,000 a week. We capitalized at $375,000, but we spent $450,000. Robbins is a difficult man to control financially while he is creating. I don't think I was a rubber stamp. Nevertheless, before the curtain went up in Detroit, I was out of pocket $75,000.

I wasn't worried. We opened in Detroit in the summer

during a newspaper strike, so there were no reviews. Still, we were a smash from the first performance. You couldn't get near the theatre. Parenthetically, the only review was a pan in *Variety,* which called the show excessively commercial, mediocre.

I wrote my investors to disregard what they might read; they had a hit. I had felt that way from the first day of rehearsal. Getting into rehearsal seems to have been our only crisis.

Gun-shy as ever, with the actors signed, the scenery being built in the shop, and only ten days to go, Robbins decided we weren't ready, that we must postpone a month. That was impossible: we had theatre contracts, bookings on the road, actors to pay. He replied he wasn't ready. In my opinion he was. The conversation was replaced by a telegram obdurately refusing to go into rehearsal. I accepted his decision, providing he sent me a check for $55,000, covering my personal liability.

Then there were phone calls, and then there was a visit from his lawyer. He was heartsick that it had come to this and did I really mean that I would sue Jerry for those expenses if he was not there for the first day of rehearsals? I said he could bloody well bet I meant it. And, he said, How could our friendship have come to this? I told him that my feelings were as hurt as Jerry's, and he went away convinced.

Rehearsals began on schedule.

They began with improvisations as they had in *West Side Story.* I remember two in particular. One took place in a white-owned bookstore in the South and involved the attempts of blacks to purchase books. A lesson in minority relations. The other took place in a concentration camp after the time covered by *Fiddler.* Again Robbins created respect in the actor for himself and for what the play was about. I borrowed liberally from the experience with *Fiddler* when I did *Cabaret.*

The title *Fiddler on the Roof* was suggested by Chagall's painting. Joe Stein then accommodated what we all thought was an intriguing title with a monologue at the beginning of the show.

Fiddler on the Roof was sold to United Artists for $2 million; which is less than was paid for *Man of La Mancha, My Fair Lady, Mame;* but the 25 per cent of the distributor's gross after recoupment of costs will more than compensate for the discrepancy.

I don't think a show will run longer than *Fiddler*'s 3242 performances on Broadway. It was like a rent-controlled apartment that you leased eight years ago. The economics were based on contracts drawn eight years earlier. Though our minimums adjusted with each new contract, our royalties remained what they were in 1964. We were able to break even on a weekly gross of $47,000. If *Fiddler* were to open today, it would take $75,000 to operate each week, and that would curtail the run by more than three years.

CHAPTER 16

Jean Anouilh is largely unappreciated in this country, primarily because his plays are "French" in the particular sense that French theatre can be as remote from ours as the Kabuki. Wordy, static, adult fairy tales, they seem to possess too soft a center for American audiences.

I was in London directing *She Loves Me* and saw a production of Anouilh's *Poor Bitos* in a small theatre club. In this instance at center the play was hard. Donald Pleasence, in the dual role of Bitos and Robespierre, gave an epic performance.

Bitos wasn't tempting to the New York importers of plays. They calculated, correctly, its dubious commercial prospects. Disregarding the obvious, I imported it because it was the most astonishing play I'd seen in too long, and I wanted even remotely to be joined to it.

In the case of *Bitos,* we rerehearsed in New York, bringing only Donald Pleasence and Charles Gray from the London company. We recreated to the last detail the London set, although the United Scenic Artists insisted that we credit an American designer who in fact did nothing more than supervise the building and the hanging of it in the theatre. I deplore anything which inhibits a free flow of creative talent between countries. Much has been said about protecting the American actor from the infiltration of the British, and vice versa, but not enough to convince me. There are periods Broadway is British and *vice versa* and over the years it comes out even.

The director was an American girl, Shirley Butler, who has since died. She duplicated the London production except for the costumes, which were designed by Donald Brooks. There was no fun in the doing of it for any of us. There rarely is in duplicating.

Pleasence, frustrated by the literalness of the original production, had hoped that when it transferred from London, it would be totally reconceived. I was quite willing to *listen* to the play. My predilection for theatricality is not exclusive. Occasionally, I like the static verbosity of French theatre.

A year later, when I saw Andre Gregory's surrealistic production at The Theatre of the Living Arts in Philadelphia, with sets, costumes, performances outsized, and the ideas at the heart of the play moving, I knew for the first time what Pleasence meant.

In the intervening years my work probably is best characterized by precisely that production Pleasence sought, but at the time I didn't know what he was talking about.

It is worth mentioning that *Bitos* sold out its two preview weeks to cheering audiences. Then we opened and the show was dismissed with faint praise by the critics, and Pleasence virtually ignored. (In *The Man in the Glass*

Booth a few seasons later, they noticed). Business stopped dead. This is partly explained by lower preview prices, making Broadway theatre available to a less-affluent intellectual segment of the audience.

After the disappointing reviews, I reduced ticket prices so that we could run on a week-to-week basis, meeting expenses, with no possibility of profit, but no one came. Two weeks later we closed.

CHAPTER 17

After *She Loves Me* there were many offers to direct musicals from other producers. Joshua Logan had agreed to direct one for Alex Cohen based on the Sherlock Holmes stories. Wisely, he changed his mind, and Alex asked me to hear the score.

I had always figured that some day I would give up producing and direct exclusively for other managements. I would put behind me advertising campaigns and theatre terms and actors' agents and union negotiations; that would be my nirvana.

The score for *Baker Street* had been written by Ray Jessel and Marian Grudeff. An audition was arranged in Marian Grudeff's apartment. I should have known from that day what trouble I was getting into. All the while Jessel, the lyricist, played the score and auditioned the material for me, Grudeff, the composer, talked through the numbers, Jerome Coopersmith, the librettist, imploring her to shut up and permit me to listen.

I admired two of the songs, but little of the rest. The

book, which I read that evening, was well constructed, nicely written, a small atmospheric show. In the script they'd cooked up an antiseptic love affair for Holmes. A bad idea. They'd cast Inga Swenson, who the previous season had knocked them dead in *110 in the Shade,* as the glamorous paramour. The lady and the love story were a part of the package. I should have known.

Baker Street could have been a one-set musical, sans love, sans chorus, the whole of it in Holmes's study with red flocked wallpaper, Victorian furniture, steaming beakers, and sliding panels.

I agreed to direct it, providing that if by Labor Day 1963 the new numbers weren't acceptable, Cohen would replace the composers with Bock and Harnick. Then I went to work with Grudeff and Jessel to try and get the score right.

In the course of a career you are afraid to work because you are afraid to fail, and alternately, you get to thinking that if you are working, you can't fail. This time the latter applied.

It is calamitous to accept inferior material. And arrogant. There are so many surprises in the making of a show, unanticipated disappointments, problems, you cannot afford to make compromises up front. Again I went to work because I wanted to work. I was easier to work with in those days, stifling demands, deferring explosion until it was too late.

By Labor Day we didn't have the required material. I asked that Bock and Harnick be brought in. I was told that Alex Cohen was committed to Grudeff and Jessel and that if I backed out now, it was too late to replace me and the rights would revert to the Conan Doyle Estate, forfeiting four years of work and massive out-of-pocket preproduction costs. Was it worth scuttling the show? I decided no it was not worth it. I was wrong. My acquiescence at a point when we might have turned it all around instead sank it. The intimate show I was planning was for the Broad*hurst* Theatre (1100); we got the Broad*way* Theatre (1800). Bring on the dancing girls, bring on the sets and costumes.

I had one good idea. The second act called for Queen Victoria's jubilee procession along The Mall to Buckingham Palace. I asked Bil Baird to build a parade of animated wooden soldiers, followed by a tiny gold coach with Victoria inside, waving a lace handkerchief. Although we had added thirty-six dancers and singers, we retained our puppets in Act II, and they walked off with the show. They showed the multimillion-dollar musical "with a cast of thousands," on the biggest stage on Broadway, what it might have been.

In this instance *Variety*, from Boston, reported we were a combination of *Around the World in Eighty Days* and *My Fair Lady*. So by the time we opened, we had that responsibility riding our backs. I hold myself responsible for the outcome. I'd backed off when I should have persisted. I don't like to fight, and when I work for myself, I don't have to. I shortchanged Cohen in my misplaced effort to be congenial.

And so my office still exists. A lot of the responsibility has been taken off my shoulders by Ruth Mitchell, my associate producer, by my general manager, Howard Haines, who succeeded Carl Fisher as general manager, by Annette Meyers, my assistant, but I know it's being done my way. Their mistakes are my mistakes.

Add to that I have a terrible fear of being replaced on a show. Since most successful musicals are in some trouble on the road, if I were working for another producer, he might get jittery and fire me. I remember telling David Merrick when he asked me to direct *Hello, Dolly!*, "You'll fire me. I can see it now in the *New York Times*. You're hiring me so you can fire me." He replied that he had never fired a director in his life. On the other hand, there's always a first time.

And too, if I gave up producing, I would be at the mercy of job offers. On Broadway, unlike in the West End, there is simply not enough work, and able directors are forced to accept inferior material in order to work. As a producer, I create my opportunities.

After *Baker Street* I was not offered another directing job for three years.

ROBERT PHILLIPS

Hal Prince, Bobby Griffith, George Abbott. DAMN YANKEES, *Adelphi Theatre (later became the George Abbott Theatre, since torn down)*

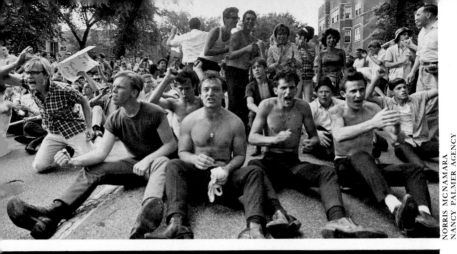

Opposite: CABARET
top: Was this Germany in the '30's?
middle: "Don't Tell Mama"
bottom: The company and the mirror

Below: COMPANY
top: Aronson's New York (½ inch model)
bottom: Inhabited, on the stage at the Alvin

BOTH PHOTOS: ROBERT GALBRAITH

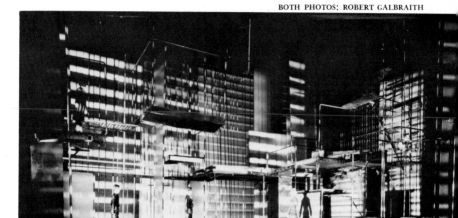

FOLLIES
Gloria Swanson in the rubble of the Roxy

ELIOT ELISOFON

The model by Aronson
ROBERT GALBRAITH

Explaining the set on the first day of rehearsal

MARTHA SWOPE

Rehearsing on set in Bronx at Feller Scenery Studios

On stage at the Winter Garden

A LITTLE NIGHT MUSIC

GREAT GOD BROWN: *Model by Aronson*

THE VISIT: *The automobile ride*

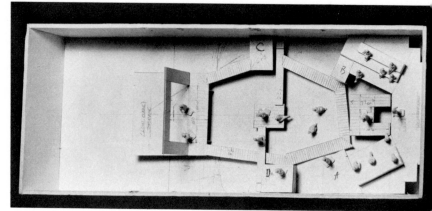

CANDIDE
top: Set model in shoebox by Eugene Lee
bottom: The Auto da Fé

CHAPTER 18

Flora, the Red Menace was the last of the plays I produced that I didn't direct. It was based on Lester Atwell's book, *Love Is Just Around the Corner,* the story of an extroverted young girl, a commercial artist, looking for work in the post-Depression years and becoming involved with the Young Communist League.

I wanted to direct that show.

Of all the shows I have done which didn't work, I regret the failure of *Flora* most especially. What it could have been! And it was the perfect time for it. Joe McCarthy was dead.

I gave it to Kander and Ebb to read. I had known them for some time individually, not as a team. They agreed to compose some songs on spec.

I asked Garson Kanin to adapt it. Instead, he recommended Robert Russell with whom he'd written one of the Tracy–Hepburn films. Russell had had personal experience with The Movement. He went to work writing with Barbra Streisand in mind.

Quite soon I realized he needed help in the craft of constructing a musical. Also, there was an obduracy, an unwillingness to bend, an impracticality, difficult to analyze. I came to think he had an uneasy compact with failure on this one, the result perhaps of his experiences during those painful years. Eager to work on the one hand, but pessimistic about the outcome. The cynic had replaced the idealist.

Anyway, we argued often, and it didn't get written. Someone had to be found, a collaborator, experienced, who could take from him the best he had to give. Who better than Abbott?

Abbott liked the novel, some of Russell's dialogue, and while he found Kander and Ebb's songs brilliant, he quarreled with the best of them on the grounds that they were overemotional, even turgid.

The title, which was Russell's, perfectly set the tone of the show. *Flora, the Red Menace.* Affectionate, somehow rueful. "Workers and peasants of Sheepshead Bay unite for bread, peace and land!"

Abbott felt the affection, but the quality of the emotion eluded him. He was born in 1886. He has lived through three wars, two police actions, the Crash, and Joe McCarthy. Just as he was about to be drafted in 1918, Armistice was declared. He predicted the Crash and was out of the market six months before it happened. He has been secure financially for over sixty years. He is essentially an apolitical man.

He brought to *Flora* no clear attitude about the Party. His Communists were cartoon characters, some of them farcical, others evil.

I wish I'd had the guts to tell him then that I wanted to direct it. He would have been surprised, but characteristically, after the surprise wore off, the idea might have appealed to him. And had we worked together, perhaps I could have created a consistent attitude toward that element in the material. Instead, I abdicated.

Abbott sent the first draft from Florida, using little of Russell's material. The best of the numbers no longer fit. So I flew down to Florida with my misgivings. He suggested that a good solution would be for Kander and Ebb to visit him there. I assumed they would stay about ten days, and during that time could persuade him to put the emotion back in the show. More specifically, to clarify our attitudes about radicals in that period.

They arrived in Florida one day, they were back in New York twenty-four hours later. Abbott had conducted his characteristic terse session: Had they understood what he wanted? Did they agree with him? (Apparently they gave him that impression.) They returned empty-handed but ecstatic, buoyed up by the assurance of the man.

Abbott's granitelike stability tranquilized them. More appropriately, they were intoxicated, and this pattern prevailed. Each time they would come to me justifiably worried about the material, I would send them to the telephone or to the typewriter to contact Abbott, and each time they would return in orbit.

As for Abbott, he wondered what all the ruckus was about. Abbott loves the life in Florida in the winter. He was willing to return in mid-February, a concession, but unwilling to spend the winter in New York with us. Clearly it was my responsibility to insist that he be here or that we postpone till the following season, which no one wanted to do. Again, what was the rush? Abbott spends his summers near New York. We could have worked the summer months together. As it was, we went into rehearsal with an incomplete script. In addition, Abbott left the supervision of the scenery and costumes to me.

Meantime, Russell was furious and verbal about it. He knew it was wrong, but he didn't know how to fix it. And because he didn't and he was the outsider, we closed ranks around Abbott. Sometimes protecting Abbott took precedence over protecting the play.

The point is, we had momentum. An opening date in April, the Alvin Theatre, and Abbott. People in the theatre overrate momentum. They worry that if they stop the engine, they will never get it going again, and too, theatre people rarely know when a show is going to work. The lady who corners you at the cocktail party and says she could have told you, just might have, given her objectivity, but doing shows is a subjective process and there is always an element of surprise for its creators when a show succeeds. Wishful thinking is built into the best of shows.

We didn't cast Barbra Streisand. She wasn't available. But Liza Minnelli was, having opened Off-Broadway in a tacky but energetic revival of *Best Foot Forward*. Just nineteen, she had a voice that reminded you of her mother, intelligence about character, and best of all for me, she moved wonderfully.

I counted *Flora* out before it opened in Boston, spending most of my time in the lobby of the Colonial Theatre. This was a step ahead of staying in bed as I did in Philadelphia with *A Swim in the Sea*. Astonishingly, it was well received in Boston, by both the critics and the public. Somewhat surprised, but happy, Abbott and his collaborators, excepting me, worked hard and well and the show improved. So much so that by the time we previewed in New York, I began to believe we had a hit.

The reviews on Broadway were awful. They needn't have been. How often before you learn the lesson?

CHAPTER 19

In 1965 I was working with Kander, Ebb, and Masteroff on *Cabaret,* but it doesn't belong here in the book because we were stymied, and *this time* I postponed.

Instead, I picked up another of David Merrick's discards, *Superman.* It was an original, written by Robert Benton and David Newman (*Bonnie and Clyde*), with a score by Strouse and Adams (*Bye Bye Birdie*). The script I optioned had been completed a year earlier and anticipated the Pop Art craze. It was old-fashioned and funny, in a wisecracking way. Dressed up in 1940s wardrobe, it would have passed in a season of *Too Many Girls* and *Panama Hattie.* The jargon was the 1960s, but there was no attempt to comment on those times. It didn't even *occur* to me that we might have.

In fact, long after the play closed Boris Aronson told me that *Superman* was the one show that he wished he'd been asked to design because it could have been the definitive contemporary musical.

The presence of Superman in a realistic musical describing the quality of urban life in the 1960s with real villains instead of mad scientists might have helped us survive the Pop Art fad which overtook us. Written in 1964, *Superman* set the style. Produced in 1965, it followed it.

I didn't enjoy working on *Superman* mostly because we opened so badly in Philadelphia. The reviews were humiliating, and there was trouble with Jack Cassidy, who was starring in a flashy but subordinate role. Because of this, I expanded the role in rehearsal to accommodate his many talents. When we opened in Philadelphia, we were long, and I began to cut, the normal way of things. But he resented these cuts terribly. For each excision he had a suggested alternative. He would whip out a scrap of paper with a new line and read it aloud in front of the entire company. I was forced each time to reject it, which didn't discourage him. Each day new scraps of paper and new jokes and the process wore us both down. In this instance I won, or I think I did, but I realized how castrating an actor can be if he chooses. We are all familiar with the occasions in which a director can bully an actor into confusion, but there are just as many times when actors run off with the play. Stars do it all the time.

Though the *New York Times* called *Superman* the best musical of that year, we couldn't compete with Batman five nights weekly on television, ZOWIE sweatshirts, and Andy Warhol. The fad had peaked, and we closed in four months.

With *Superman* Ruth Mitchell, my right hand, became an associate producer, in charge of all technical elements of the productions, and I never worried about them again.

Almost imperceptibly, she also moved into the role of an assistant director.

As in *Flora,* there was another show in *Superman,* but I had neither the self-confidence nor *comprehension* of what I might bring to the work of other people. The trouble is, everything the show might have been became clear after I'd done it. A concept, a point of view emerged after the work. That was because I had not yet begun to think of myself as a director. It was a costly way to learn.

CHAPTER 20

Gwen Verdon and Tammy Grimes had both been mentioned for musical versions of *I Am a Camera*. Sandy Wilson (*The Boy Friend*) wrote the book, music, and lyrics for one to star Julie Andrews, and for a time she was interested.

What drew me to *Cabaret* had very little to do with Sally Bowles. I say *Cabaret* rather than *I Am a Camera* because ultimately we used Christopher Isherwood's *Berlin Stories* to step off from. What attracted the authors and me was the parallel between the spiritual bankruptcy of Germany in the 1920s and our country in the 1960s. The assassinations of Martin Luther King and Medgar Evers, the march on Selma, the murder of the three young men, Goodman, Chaney, and Schwerner.

To implement our point of view, on the first day of rehearsal, borrowing from Robbins' technique, I produced a centerfold from *Life* magazine of August 19, 1966, of a group of Aryan blonds in their late teens, stripped to the waist, wearing religious medals, snarling at the camera like a pack of hounds. I asked the cast to identify the time and place of the picture. It seemed obvious I'd lifted it from Munich in 1928. In fact, it was a photograph of a group of students in residential Chicago fighting the integration of a school.

I went so far in one draft of the show to end it with film of the march on Selma and the Little Rock riots, but that was a godawful idea, and I came to my senses.

Calling it *Cabaret* was Joe Masteroff's idea. The life of the cabaret, a metaphor for Germany. In his first draft he and Kander and Ebb experimented with two scores running concurrently, one within the book for the personae; the other pastiche for the entertainers. But who were to be the entertainers? A dancing chorus was predictable and difficult to give dimension to. Sally had been a lousy singer, so there was some question about how much lousy singing you wanted to impose on the show.

(When we got around to casting Sally Bowles, Kander and Ebb opted for Liza Minnelli, an idea I summarily rejected. She wasn't British—I'm not sure why that was important to me—and she sang too well; I still think that was a flaw in the film.)

Then I remembered that when I was stationed with the army near Stuttgart in 1951, there was a nightclub called Maxim's in the rubble of an old church basement. Whenever possible I hung out in Maxim's. There was a dwarf MC, hair parted in the middle and lacquered down with brilliantine, his mouth made into a bright-red cupid's bow, who wore heavy false eyelashes and sang, danced, goosed, tickled, and pawed four lumpen Valkyres waving diaphanous butterfly wings.

The show started naturalistically in the compartment

of a train with the arrival of the leading man in Berlin. Immediately it was to be followed by a "turn," six or eight songs fragmented to introduce Berlin night life and to be performed by my MC from Maxim's, making quick changes from Lenya to Richard Tauber to Dietrich, and so on.

I arranged an audition for Joel Grey, who immediately caught the component courage, self-delusion, fear, and sadness of this mediocre MC. He didn't bother with the Germanness.

For a short time we had two shows. A predictable realistic telling of the writer's encounter with Sally, and Joel Grey's fifteen minutes. Instead, we took Joel's numbers and scattered them through the show in an ascending curve energetically and descending curve morally. He opened effortfully, empty laughter to an empty house. He'd lost the war, his self-respect. He carried his money around in bushel baskets. With National Socialism he found his strength, misdirected and despotic, feeding off his moral corruption. In those eight numbers the MC became the metaphor.

It was a good idea, but only half a concept. What would it look like? How would it happen? I had no idea. I postponed and did *Superman* instead.

In the spring *Superman* opened and closed, and I went to Russia to get away from it and the insoluble problems of *Cabaret*.

In Moscow I attended the Taganka Theatre's *Ten Days That Shook the World*, a political revue suggested by John Reed's book. I had been touted onto it, and had ordered and paid for the tickets well in advance. When I went to pick them up, I was told the Young Communists had taken the entire theatre and my money was refunded. I made an awful scene (in Russia scenes are often the only means of getting things done, and upon advice, this one was coldly premeditated), saying I had come all the way to Russia to see that production, then enlisted help at the American Embassy, ultimately receiving two seats in the last row of the balcony. Luckily, it was a small theatre.

I mention this because had I not gone, I would have missed out on a theatrical experience I count a turning point in my thinking as a director. Part cabaret theatre, Taganka borrows liberally from the Russian actor-director Vsevolod Meyerhold, who began with Stanislavsky at the Moscow Art Theatre and broke away on his own in protest of the extreme realism of that movement, exploring instead means of using theatre techniques to excite, creating an audience of participants in which subjective involvement was all.

I'd been raised in a fairly conventional musical theatre. Even *West Side Story,* which had the audacity to contain that much dance and to move that much ahead with each dance, without words, explosive as the whole concept was, was not something new. It was the pinnacle of a tradition.

In 1964 Joan Littlewood's *Oh, What a Lovely War!* had fractured the musical form into something resembling a revue, discarding central characters, a story line. A couple of seasons earlier her *Fings Ain't What They Used To Be* explored less successfully ways of shaking up an audience by taking the predictability out of the experience.

Still until that night at the Taganka, I believed the most important element of a musical to be the book. The score was secondary. A rule and as such, no more valid than the reverse, which is subscribed to by most of my peers.

The text of *Ten Days* was absurd. Trenchant political satire in Moscow in 1966 exploited the villainy of Alexander Kerensky and Woodrow Wilson. But the techniques, the vitality, the imagination to make every minute surprising, *involving,* yet consistent with a concept are the stock in trade of this theatre.

Ten Days began in the lobby, spilled across the stage into the audience, shattering the fourth wall. Nothing new in that: musicals always break the wall. Actors step down, turn front and sing. But there are ways and ways to break walls.

The Taganka was conventional in that there was the stage, the proscenium, the orchestra pit, the auditorium: nothing environmental about it. However, there were technical devices which knocked me out. An apron built out over the orchestra pit into which searchlights were sunk. These lights, slanted over the heads of the audience to the last row in the balcony, when lighted, instead of blinding, became a curtain of light behind which the scenery was changed. Paintings on the wall spoke, inanimate objects animated, disembodied hands, feet, and faces washed across the stage. There were puppets and projections, front and rear, and the source and colors of light were always a surprise. All of it made possible by the use of black velours drapes instead of painted canvas. I date my love affair with black velours from that performance.

Each of these ideas capitalized on the special relationship of live actors and live observers. It is that relationship which is exclusively ours in the theatre. Film and television cannot touch it. And properly appreciated, it gives us the chance to make connections, to string unseen emotional bands between actor and audience. The business of physical contact is the least of it.

Old techniques? Probably. But I had never seen them used so well. They affected me like a shot of adrenalin.

A few seasons later the Taganka's production of *Hamlet* worked brilliantly. They used a length of fabric strung from guy wires, which, moving in any direction on the stage, suggested a wall, a piece of furniture, a door, the exterior of a castle, or Gertrude's closet. Ingmar Bergman used something of the sort in the National Theatre's production of *Hedda Gabler*. Effortlessly, the actors moved a blood-red screen, about the size of a door and mounted on casters, to divide rooms, to construct unseen walls, to isolate the interior workings of a character's mind from his external behavior.

I came home and called Jean Rosenthal, who was going to light the show, describing for her what I'd seen. I asked her to give me a curtain of light so we could change scenery behind it. She informed me that there's no equipment in the world powerful enough to accomplish what I wanted in a Broadway theatre. The throw from the source of the light to the back wall wouldn't be intense enough.

Scrap that idea. Come up with another.

I suggested splitting the stage in two: an area to represent the REAL WORLD, the vestibule in Sally's rooming house, her bedroom, the train, the cabaret; and an area to represent the MIND. Joel Grey's material was divided between realistic numbers performed in the cabaret for an audience on stage and metaphorical numbers illustrating changes in the German mind. We called this the Limbo Area.

Jean designed a light trough about six feet upstage of the edge of the apron. Covered with a wooden shield, it rose electronically and could be directed at an angle of forty-five degrees upstage to the rear wall (we danced a Tiller Chorus of lumpen Valkyres across the stage, lighting only their legs). Downstage at forty-five degrees we momentarily blinded the audience. And at ninety degrees straight up into the flies we made a curtain of dust.

Our trough served as footlights for the MC. Five waiters singing "Tomorrow Belongs to Me" stepped across it and disappeared upstage. At the climax of the show, Sally Bowles sang "Cabaret," lost track of her audience, broke down, and for the first time in the evening, stepped across the footlights into the Limbo Area, and the audience understood.

So much for the lighting.

Boris Aronson is a good talker. He has a quirky and penetrating vision of people, time, and place. His analysis of a news event, of conflict in fiction, invariably surprises. He possesses an extraordinary, active vocabulary. (He has been writing a book for years. I wish he'd finish it so I can read it.)

Cabaret was the first of our collaborations. We talked for three months, rarely of things visual, mostly of the characters, false motivations, interpersonal behavior, people in different countries, ethnic peculiarities, emotional expression as affected by national or ethnic considerations. Of course, he collected thousands of photographs, but he never observed the predictable: never the leg of a table, the shape of a lamp post, the ironwork on the hotel balcony rail. Rather, he would call my attention to the expression of the shoppers on the street, to the quality of light in a room, the emotional content in the architecture of a section of the city.

Boris puts great store in his opinion of material. He's right. Also, he makes problems or unearths them and worries them to death. He's not negative; he is troublesome. When Boris talks, I hear and see things I neither heard nor saw before.

Just about when you've run out of talk and you think it's time he went to work, he presents you with a finished design. Apparently he has been working on versions of it all along. Though his renderings in watercolor and gouache are beautiful works of art, he always does a quarter-inch scale model. From this we make whatever changes are necessary (in Boris's case, they are very few): differences in the relationship of furniture, the shape of a roof, the adjustment of doors and windows, that sort of thing. Nothing major. Once those details are taken care of, he constructs a half-inch scale model for the scenic builders and the stage managers and for me to live with and to show the actors on the first day of rehearsals. The pieces in this model are large enough to remove and hold in your hand, detailed, finely realized down to the texture of wallpaper, the design of a stained-glass window.

The model I saw of *Cabaret* was of a slightly raked stage with three black velours drapes, two on either side of the stage running slightly diagonally upstage to the third, which formed the rear wall. The side velours were rigged to fly quickly, letting the scenery roll in on winch-operated trucks. Overhead there hung two strings of street lights, built in perspective, and the tangled lines of a trolley. The lighting equipment against the black drops made it possible for Jean Rosenthal to design subtle, realistic lighting for the book scenes and to give the cabaret and Limbo numbers the hard, sinister edge of spotlights.

In addition, there was the *Cabaret* sign in neon—Joe Masteroff's idea—which opened and closed the show.

Boris designed an iron staircase typical of those backstage in nightclubs, and he put it in the Limbo Area of the stage. I had not asked for it, but it was there, and I placed ladies of the chorus on it, observing the realistic scenes of the play, and as they lit their cigarettes they cast empty eyes on the events of the play. Their indifference generated a curious dynamic to the scenes. They became the surrogate German population. This was the first time I played around with observers on stage.

In the scale model Boris surprised me with a mirror, a trapezoid, corresponding to the shape of the stage floor, suspended above the center of the stage and slanted to reflect the audience. It cast an additional, uneasy metaphor over the evening.

Apropros surprises, there are always surprises from Boris. In *Company* it was the two elevators. In *Night Music* the plastic trees.

Fred Ebb recommended Ron Field as choreographer. Although I had never seen his work, I had no other enthusiasms, so I agreed. I imagine that seems an unprofessional way to make such an important decision, but we had come by Bob Fosse on *Pajama Game* exactly the same way. The point is, Ron Field had the experience and when we talked, he had the enthusiasm.

Cabaret was an enormous amount of work for him and each of the numbers required an idea, and he seemed to have good ideas to waste.

Later, we did *Zorba* together and then he began to direct, and was especially successful with *Applause,* but he succumbed to the glamor and insistent pressures of Hollywood and moved there to choreograph films, television specials, and Las Vegas club acts. Apparently it is impossible to resist those temptations.

I am happy to say that he has since moved back to New York, back to the theatre. Isn't it paradoxical that television film stars visiting New York (to present Tony Awards?) seem awed by the stage while Broadway people can't wait to drop everything and move to California?

Because the shape of *Cabaret* had taken an unconventional turn, because we were experimenting with alien theatrical devices, we determined to move away from Isherwood's material. The *Berlin Stories,* from which *I Am a Camera* was written, are about Sally Bowles's "scandalous" relationship with a homosexual writer. Plotless, really, there are events along the way, but essentially they are a pair of character studies with ominous presentiments of anti-Semitism just offstage in the wings. We persuaded ourselves that the musical comedy audience required a sentimental heterosexual love story with a beginning, middle, and end to make the concept palatable.

Not content with that, we added Lotte Lenya and Jack Gilford in a subordinate love story. The structure, indeed familiar: Ado Annie and Will Parker, Hineszie and Gladys, Adelaide and Nathan Detroit.

In my opinion we were wrong. The plotless musical might not have worked, but had it, the whole project would have been consistent with its aspirations. If we had *Cabaret* to do all over again, I believe we would have made the audacious choice. In defense, it was 1966. A lot has happened since then, and so quickly that the film, in 1972, dealt explicitly with homosexuality. I liked that part of the film; I missed the metaphoric use of the MC.

Re the presence of sufficient conventional elements to make a show comfortable for its audience: *West Side Story, Company,* and *Follies* didn't sell out; *Cabaret* did.

Just before we left for Boston, I ran separate performances of *Cabaret,* one for George Abbott and one for Steve Sondheim. They are the two I most like to hear from at that stage. They never waste your time with the obvious; they figure you see it and you'll get around to it in good time. But also they edit out anything impractical, because your scenery won't accommodate it, or your cast can't handle it, or you haven't the time for it.

Soon after we'd opened in Boston one suggestion kept cropping up from friends, but also from strangers who write letters knowing you are fixing. I resisted it until everything else was in place and the show had found steady legs. I learned from Abbott and Robbins that you can do almost anything drastic when the show is cut, there are no more lines to learn, and the performances are secure.

In this case, the pressure was to take "Cabaret" from the end of the show and use it to introduce Sally Bowles. This meant replacing her first song, "Don't Tell Mama," with "Cabaret" and replacing "Cabaret" with a marvelous Kander and Ebb song, "I Don't Care Much," which had been written for the show and never used.

My instincts were against it, but because it had been suggested so many times, I was dying to see what would happen. Three days before the opening in New York, Goddard Lieberson, in charge of Columbia Records, begged me to try it. I asked Jill Haworth, who was playing Sally Bowles, whether she was willing to learn a brand-new song that close to the reviews. She agreed. It went in that night and destroyed the show. The climactic moment of *Cabaret* was half as effective with the new song. The song, coming at the top of the show, went by unnoticed; the giddiness of "Don't Tell Mama" was missing. It was as though we had leveled the emotions of the show across the board.

Something like this happened with *Pajama Game*. Jerry Robbins had always wanted "Seven and a Half Cents" to open the show. Acting on instinct, Abbott resisted until a New York preview and then tried it. The number, which had been affectionately humorous at the end of the show, was serious business in front. It scared the hell out of Abbott, and he refused to try it for a second performance.

Twelve years later I put things back the way they were —fast.

In the second act of *Cabaret* Joel Grey sang a love song to a gorilla wearing a pink tutu and carrying a purse. "If You Could See Her Through My Eyes" was sweet and funny, except for the final line in which he looked at her and sang, "If you could see her through my eyes, she wouldn't look Jewish at all." Some laughed, most were shocked, many were offended. It was as we intended, but that didn't matter. We began receiving letters of protest from individuals in the audience, and in time from rabbis and entire congregations. After the first New York preview, the audience stayed to argue in the theatre, sizable segments on either side heatedly debating the propriety of it.

I introduced myself to them and after listening to both sides, called the authors together. We talked. A sleepless night later I made Ebb change the last line in the lyric, and I emasculated the song.

The company was upset. So was I, but not as upset as they. Fred Ebb still hasn't forgotten it. Ebb: "I've never known you to pander to the public." But I was right. I didn't want the show closing over that.

When we did the show in London, we put the lyric back and the letters followed. And we took the line out.

When the film was made, they put the line in, but shot a number of alternatives and showed them at sneak previews. Finally, they took it out.

The success of *Cabaret* at the box office made the difference. I was offered plays to direct for other people.

Had I done *Cabaret* as I would do it now, would those who felt we had compromised have liked it? Probably. But my shows don't do as well now at the box office as *Cabaret* did because now I do them exactly as I want to do them. It has cost me something, and the price at the moment isn't too high.

CHAPTER 21

Herschel Bernardi had the idea to musicalize the Kazant-zakis novel *Zorba the Greek,* and he and Joe Stein brought it to me. Michael Cacoyannis' recent film was filled with exciting music and dance, and I was attracted to it philosophically. The novel multiplied my enthusiasm. Kander and Ebb shared it.

Maria Karnilova was our instant choice for Bouboulina, the part that Lila Kedrova played so well on the screen.

It all fell into place.

The public wanted to see it. The benefit party ladies wanted to sell it. Our advance sale, sans advertising, reached $2 million.

It fell exactly into that category of shows I said I would never do, a show so anticipated that it must disappoint. And that's what happened to *Zorba.*

Even the concept came easily. We would translate the traditional Greek chorus into a group of musicians I had seen in a bouzouki restaurant near Piraeus. Thirty-eight men and women sitting in a semicircle, each holding a musical instrument, dressed in the gaudiest of makeshift costumes with spangles, smoking, talking, singing solos or in unison, interrupting each other with horseplay and laughter.

Our play began in the present and the company took us back forty years to introduce Zorba in a similar café on the waterfront. Assuming all the roles, they used their chairs and props to imagine a waiting room on a dock, and their musical instruments to create the sounds of the wind and the sea, and scraps of material from the women's skirts suggested costumes.

Boris's basic unit was the classic Greek amphitheatre with levels in a semicircle. Onto these levels he introduced fragments of scenery, an olive tree, the entrance to a church, a restaurant, a store, a balcony, and by the third scene in the play we'd constructed a realistic village in Crete, made of molded styrofoam, and climbing the side of a hill. By then the entire company was realistically costumed.

The trouble is that we had turned our backs on the imagination we had displayed in the opening, and by the second act were defeated by the degree of realism we had achieved in the first. There is a mine disaster, important to the plot of *Zorba*. In the film it was elaborately enacted on a real mountain with tons of explosives and hundreds of extras. We attempted a similar effect with two smoke pots, a taped explosion, and thirty-eight people running here and there, simulating terror.

The mine disaster was endemic to the plot. Had we

acknowledged the limitations of the stage, we might have made capital of the mine disaster. Dance might have worked, though I'm tired of it. There had to be something imaginative, but we were stuck with realism, and what was worse, we couldn't keep the events offstage.

As for the casting, it was one of those educated guesses. Beware of those. Bernardi and Karnilova had played Tevye and Golde a year earlier. Apparently I was counting on the audience wanting to see "the Lunts" playing totally different characters. I was wrong. And the casting created unnecessary comparisons with *Fiddler*.

I think *Zorba* was a first-rate, if depressing, show. What exhilarated me evidently depressed others. The opening number was called "Life Is What You Do While You're Waiting To Die." Arthur Laurents said that sank us.

In *Zorba* Boris and I got to know a great deal more about each other again. We did more thinking about the space than we had before. The palette: the blacks, the grays, the whites, how to work with them. We did more experimentation: the business of having people stand around and observe and comment, be within the story and without it, touched on in *Cabaret,* amplified subsequently in *Company* and *Follies*.

There was a ballad in the second act of *Zorba* in which a young man sings to the woman he loves, and it becomes a trio as a lady representing the Greek chorus observes the scene and joins in. I never got it to work.

In *Follies* several years later I had a man sing to an apparition of a young girl he'd been in love with thirty years earlier, while her counterpart, the woman she'd grown up to be, stood by and mistook his song as being sung to her. Two women and a man, essentially the staging quite the same. In *Follies* I knew how to make it work.

So you learn. Boris said *Follies* would not have happened had it not been for *Cabaret, Zorba,* and *Company*.

Zorba closed prematurely because Bernardi and Karnilova got to fighting. Personal difficulties in Bernardi's life contributed to physical problems, and he began to miss performances. It was catching: Karnilova matched him performance for performance, and soon both stars were out.

Zorba was a disappointment for all of us. Our New Haven notices were marvelous, and we all thought we had another *Fiddler*. The *New York Times* and *Daily News* reviews were excellent, but it never happened. Each day the advance diminished.

Sometimes it's easier to close a flop, harder to live with a borderline case. *Zorba* hung on without either joy or relief. By the summer with both stars out, I had no stomach for replacing them. Instead, we closed *Zorba* and produced two new companies. One for the Civic Light Opera in Los Angeles with John Raitt and Barbara Baxley, the other to tour, starring Michael Kermoyan and the unlikely but appropriately cast Vivian Blaine.

Zorba went on to run over a year out of town, but it never paid off its investment. It still owes its investors 26 per cent, which I think will dribble in slowly but surely, and if we all live long enough, will pay off.

It's interesting that *Zorba* has had rather more life in Europe than in this country, and that has to do with the prevailing blackness of its mood, its European acceptance of mortality. I loved it at the Theatre an der Wien in Vienna. It was also a success in the Scandinavian countries, particularly Finland, where there were four companies playing simultaneously.

CHAPTER 22

George Furth, the actor, had written eleven one-act plays. Under the title *Company,* they were to be presented by another management in New York, starring Kim Stanley, as an evening of straight plays. There was nothing connective about them except the presence of this one glorious lady.

Sondheim, a friend of Furth's, felt there was something wrong with the scheme and asked whether Furth would object to sending the plays to me for advice.

I was knocked out by them, seeing a potential musical which could examine attitudes toward marriage, the influence upon it of life in the cities, and collateral problems of especial interest to those of us in our forties.

I suggested this much to Steve over the telephone, and he agreed to do it. Just like that.

He was working on a show, *The Girls Upstairs,* with James Goldman. Joe Hardy was set to direct it, and they had scheduled rehearsals for the fall of 1970. *Company* would follow in the spring of 1971. All this, assuming Furth liked the idea.

A meeting was set, and I outlined a kind of freewheeling, unconventional musical, borrowing from the revue form and lifting those of Furth's plays dealing with marriage. We needed a central character to catalyze the partners in the marriages and to connect the disparate episodes. We invented a single man, and Steve baptized him Robert, so that he could be referred to differently by each of his friends. In other words, "Bobby," "Bubbi," "Baby," "Robbie," "Rob," and so on.

If in fact it could be a musical, how to make it one? The real problem was, the plays stood on their own. Interruptions by musical numbers would kill their pace. Thirteen love songs wouldn't do, nor would thirteen marriage songs. The problem in the theatre occasionally creates the marvelous solution. In this instance, Sondheim left the plays intact and composed a score for those members of the company not involved in a specific episode. The observers.

Still we lacked a unifying concept. Just as Steve needed an excuse to write the score, I needed an excuse to move the people.

We retained three of the original short plays. Furth adapted a fourth and wrote a fifth. At this point we had five married couples and Robert. George invented three single girls to keep Robert happy—or confused—or single. Those fourteen people comprised the entire company, still another play on the title.

I suggested ours be an "acting" company, fourteen individuals to assume the roles of married people only when we needed them. They would move the furniture and props around the stage: they would be required to inhabit the stage, for the length of the show. Each would have one costume with perhaps a few accessories.

It didn't turn out that way, but that is how we started.

From the first, Boris and I wanted as spare a production as possible: a couple of tables, half a dozen chairs, a bench, some pots and pans, cups and glasses, and a bed. We agreed that Boris would design a structure encompassing five separate rooms. These would be interchangeable. The bedroom for one couple became the kitchen for another, the nursery for one, the library for another. The couples would move from room to room in the course of living even the mundane moments of their lives. And the decor in each room would identify its married couple.

To focus our attention on a particular couple, we would reproduce their room—center and stage level. As if that weren't enough, company numbers ("What Would We Do Without You?") would be performed on the entire unit without any scenery.

Complicated? So complicated that we abandoned it.

I was filming *Something for Everyone* in Germany that summer. Toward the end of July, Steve phoned from New York that there were problems with *The Girls Upstairs,* that the director wanted a good deal more rewriting, and the producer, Stuart Ostrow, was determined to postpone until the spring; in other words, *Company's* dates.

The idea of being without a show the next season upset me. I'd worked quickly with Furth and Sondheim, Boris was in the throes of designing, I'd booked theatres in Boston and New York, and even cast Elaine Stritch—all of this in less than three months. I refused to postpone. We had a contract and I was going to hold him to it.

Steve said he felt as if he were giving birth to a stillborn child. He and Goldman had worked five years on *The Girls Upstairs,* and he didn't see how he could write *Company* in his present state of depression.

I sympathized but refused the postponement, reasoning that any solutions which had eluded them for five years weren't going to appear miraculously with an additional six months. And if there was to be no *Company* in January, then there would be no *Girls Upstairs* either. Steve, who hadn't been heard on Broadway since *Anyone Can Whistle* and was looking forward to two shows in the one season, suddenly was faced with the probability of none. I knew of no other way to deal with it.

With the problem still up in the air, Steve appeared in Europe with three songs for *Company.* The first of them, "Company," is probably the best song in the score. Talk about setting the ground rules for the evening, the style, "Company" does it perfectly.

The second number, "The Little Things You Do Together," was written for Elaine Stritch and the company and established the technique of characters observing in song the non-musical material.

The third, written for Robert at the end of the show, expressed the opinion that living with someone is hell, but living alone is impossible. "Marry Me a Little" was brilliant and harshly cynical. Robert had covered no distance, learned nothing in the course of the evening. He would marry someone and they would go their separate ways, which isn't exactly what we had set out to say about marriage.

MARRY ME A LITTLE *

Marry me a little,
Love me just enough.
Cry, but not too often,
Play, but not too rough.
Keep a tender distance,
So we'll both be free.
That's the way it ought to be.
I'm ready!

Marry me a little,
Do it with a will.
Make a few demands
I'm able to fulfill.
Want me more than others,
Not exclusively.
That's the way it ought to be,
I'm ready!
I'm ready now!

You can be my best friend.
I can be your right arm.
We'll go through a fight or two,
No harm,
No harm.

We'll look not too deep,
We'll go not too far.
We won't have to give up a thing,
We'll stay who we are,
Right?
Okay, then,

I'm ready!
I'm ready now!

Someone,
Marry me a little,
Love me just enough.
Warm and sweet and easy,
Just the simple stuff.
Keep a tender distance
So we'll both be free.
That's the way it ought to be.
I'm ready!

Marry me a little,
Body, heart, and soul
Passionate as hell,
But always in control.
Want me first and foremost,
Keep me company.
That's the way it ought to be.
I'm ready!
I'm ready now!

Oh, how gently we'll talk,
Oh, how softly we'll tread.
All the stings, the ugly things
We'll keep unsaid.
We'll build a cocoon of love and respect.
You promise whatever you like,
I'll never collect.

Right?
Okay, then,
I'm ready!
I'm ready now!

Amy,
I'm ready!

There are those admirers of *Company* who refuse to believe we intended the show to be pro marriage. I assure them not only was that our avowed purpose, but to this day we regard it as a fervent plea for interpersonal relationships.

For those who still consider it an indictment, I can only drag out the old defense that some people are simply afraid to acknowledge the manifest difficulties of living together.

Anyway, if you have read the lyric above, you see why we jettisoned it. (Replacing that song remained the major musical problem, one we never entirely solved.)

What to do about *The Girls Upstairs* still faced us, so I agreed to do it (I had little idea how at the time), providing we postponed until Steve finished *Company*.

Company was the first musical I had done without conventional plot or subplot structure. The first without the hero and heroine, without the comic relief couple. There are, of course, plots, but they are subtextual and grow out of subconscious behavior, psychological stresses, inadvertent revelations: the nature of the lie people accept to preserve their relationship.

We constructed a framework of gatherings for Robert's thirty-fifth birthday, each appearing to be the same, but dynamically different from the others. Pinteresque in feeling, the first was giddy, somewhat hysterical; the second (at the end of Act I), an abbreviated version of the first; the third, hostile and staccato; and the final one at the end of the show, warm, loving, mature. Since Robert never arrives for the final celebration, there was some question whether they represented one birthday or a succession of them. I am certain they were one. I wouldn't be surprised if George Furth believes there were four. It doesn't matter.

About this time Michael Bennett agreed to stage the numbers and choreograph the dances. There was to be one professional dancer drawn from Robert's girl friends. As it turned out, there was one dance for one dancer.

Everyone in the company had to sing, after a fashion; everyone had to dance, after a fashion. But as they were to be real people, their footwork and voices were subordinated to their performances. Which is not to say some didn't sing well or move well. Some moved with agility just as some of your living-room friends move with agility, but others were klutzes and we wanted that.

We used four singers in the pit to augment the voices on stage, a technique borrowed from *Promises, Promises* and suggested by Michael Bennett and Jonathan Tunick, who orchestrated *Company*. Pit singers, serving as surrogate musical instruments, supplemented the orchestra some of the time, and some of the time the singers on stage.

Company was a heavy show, difficult to assemble. To create the illusion of spareness required six tons of steel, two electric SCR motorized elevators, and twenty-eight carousel projectors.

Most of the front projections operated from the balcony rail and the balance from X-rays on the front light pipe behind the proscenium. These were abstractions designed to support the emotions of scenes. Occasionally they contradicted the apparent mood, illuminating instead the undercurrents. The remaining slides were projected from the rear. For the scenes we used black-and-white photographs in some detail of locations in New York City; for the songs we used reverse negatives of the photographs, painted in color. There were six hundred slides in all, and most people weren't aware of them, which is as it should be.

Our projections were designed by Robert Ornbo of Theatre Projects London, and I think up until *Company* opened, projections had never been used as well on Broadway.

Company was well cast. We made no replacements on the road, which is unusual. The material adapts to many different personalities—all excepting Stritch's role, which was written for her.

When we played our first public performance in Boston, following six weeks of rehearsal, *Company* was serious business. Our cast of predominantly actors who could sing, played the results, the motivations, the subtext, let the dark, neurotic side of their characters dominate, overwhelming the comedy. The next day I suggested they take everything they'd learned about their characters, turn it upside down, and let the comedy rise to the surface. At the next performance everything was where it should be. Good material warrants that approach. It's difficult to direct comedy from the outside in. In addition, remember that material with that much subtext will vary greatly in terms of audience response. Occasionally, they didn't laugh at *Company,* but still it worked.

In rehearsal we'd replaced "Marry Me a Little" with "Happily Ever After." Steve had produced a lyric which intended to say that Robert was lying, that what we were observing was empty bravura, but the audience took him at face value, and the statement as defeatist.

HAPPILY EVER AFTER *

Someone to hold you too close,
Someone to hurt you too deep,
Someone to love you too hard,
Happily ever after.

Someone to need you too much,
Someone to read you too well,
Someone to bleed you of all the things
You don't want to tell.
That's happily ever after,
Ever, ever, ever after—
In hell.

Somebody always there
Sitting in the chair
Where you want to sit,
Always, always.
Somebody always there
Wanting you to share
Just a little bit
Always, always.

Then see the pretty girls
Smiling everywhere
From the ads and the TV set,
And why should you sweat?
What do you get?
One day of grateful
For six of regret—
With

Someone to hold you too close,
Someone to hurt you too deep,
Someone to bore you to death,
Happily ever after.
Someone you have to know well,
Someone you have to show how,
Someone you have to allow
The things you'd never allow.
That's happily ever after,
Ever, ever, ever after,
Till now.

Quick! get a little car,
Take a little drive,
Make a little love,
See a little flick,
Do a little work,
Take a little walk,
Watch a little TV
And click!
Make a little love,
Do a little work,
Get a little drunk,
You've got one little trip,
Seventy years,
Spread it around,
Take your pick:
Buy a little here,
Spend a little there,
Smoke a little pot for a little kick,
Waste a little time,
Make a little love,
Show a little feeling
But why should you try?

Why not, sure,
Feel a little lonely but fly?
Why not fly
With

No one to hold you too close,
No one to hurt you too deep,
No one to love you too hard,
Happily ever after?
No one you have to know well,
No one you have to show how,
No one you have to allow
The things you'd never allow.
That's
Happily ever after,
Ever, ever, ever after
For now.

Ever, ever, ever after. . .
Ever, ever, ever, ever ever after. . .
Ever, ever, ever after. . .

Steve wrote the third and final version of Robert's song
our last week in Boston.

BEING ALIVE *

Someone to hold you too close,
Someone to hurt you too deep,
Someone to sit in your chair,
To ruin your sleep. . .

Someone to need you too much,
Someone to know you too well
Someone to pull you up short
And put you through hell. . .

Someone you have to let in.
Someone whose feelings you spare,
Someone who, like it or not, will want you to share
A little a lot. . .

Someone to crowd you with love,
Someone to force you to care,
Someone to make you come through
Who'll always be there, as frightened as you
Of being alive,
Being alive, being alive, being alive. . .

Somebody hold me too close,
Somebody hurt me too deep,
Somebody sit in my chair
And ruin my sleep and make me aware
Of being alive, being alive.

Somebody need me too much,
Somebody know me too well,
Somebody pull me up short
And put me through hell and give me support
For being alive, make me alive
Make me alive,

Make me confused, mock me with praise,
Let me be used, vary my days.
But alone is alone, not alive.

Somebody crowd me with love,
Somebody force me to care,

Somebody let me come through,
I'll always be there as frightened as you,
To help us survive
Being alive, being alive, being alive.

I am afraid it imposed a happy ending on a play which should have remained ambiguous. A number of the musicals I have done (*She Loves Me, Company, Follies*) court ambiguity. "The Lady or the Tiger?" thrills me, but people who go to theatre are frustrated by it.

By and large, the reviews were excellent except for the *New York Times*'s. Clive Barnes didn't like the show, didn't understand it, although he said he liked it better than *West Side Story* (a line we appropriated.). Walter Kerr *admired* the show but didn't like it a hell of a lot. It was too cold for him. *I* think *Company* is warm-hearted, not sentimental, but warm-hearted.

The real impact came from the news magazines. *Time* and *Newsweek* loved it.

We had problems with our star, Dean Jones. He had been signed for a year and was increasingly unhappy in Boston. I hoped that success in New York would appease him, but as we approached Broadway, he became ill, and that illness I suspected was psychosomatic. I reasoned that the best way to insure an opening night would be to offer to replace him after we opened. Would the knowledge that he was leaving free him to give a good performance? It would and he did. And I replaced him with Larry Kert two weeks later. Business was not affected by the change. I don't know whether I would have been so generous had I thought it would be.

Excepting its final moments, *Company* represents the first time I had worked without conscious compromise. It represents as total a collaboration of authors, director, choreographer, and actors as I can remember. *Cabaret* established me as commercially successful. *Company* established me in my own eyes.

Company never played a sold-out week, often played to only 60 per cent of capacity, but it paid off and shows a profit. And that is what commercial theatre must ask of itself.

CHAPTER 23

The Girls Upstairs was a totally realistic musical about two girls and the two fellows they had married thirty years earlier, meeting at a real party in a real theatre, with real decorations and real food and drink. It dealt with the loss of innocence in the United States, using the Ziegfeld Follies (a pretty girl is *no longer* like a melody) as its metaphor.

The extent of its realism diminished its size, reduced its four leading characters to selfish overindulged pains in the neck; whereas they might have represented the misplaced American dream. (We never really licked that problem.)

I began looking for a concept. In *The Best Remaining Seats,* a history in photographs and text of the great movie palaces of the 1930s, there appeared a photograph, originally published in *Life* magazine, of Gloria Swanson standing in the rubble of what had been the Roxy Theatre. She had opened the Roxy in a silent film, and when they tore it down, Eliot Elisofon photographed her in a black chiffon dress against the gutted proscenium. A very glamorous photograph. Elisofon had captured the meta-phor.

About the same time I arranged a screening of *8½* for Michael Bennett and Ruth Mitchell. It was a first viewing for them, the ninth for me. Some years earlier a repre-sentative of Fellini's had sought me out to ask whether I would be interested in musicalizing *8½*. The movie is a masterpiece, and I was flattered and tempted, but came to realize soon that it represented Fellini's autobiography and not mine.

The Girls Upstairs dealt with aspects of character and relationships which, while not autobiographical, were in-tensely familiar. Its hero, Ben Stone, is the perfect 1970s monolith approaching menopause on the cusp of a nervous breakdown. Little wonder that I was reminded of *8½*.

The relationship with Michael Bennett on *Company* was so profitable creatively, and stimulating and easy for both of us, that I suggested he do *The Girls Upstairs* when we got around to it. He declined, feeling that he was at the point in his career when he should be directing. Soon it became more and more obvious that there was enough at least for two directors, and so I asked him whether he would like to share the assignment. A difficult arrangement for two giant egos. And there were conflicts, but never with respect to what we wanted the evening to be, to say, nor of the quality of its theatricality.

It was to be surrealistic, inspired by *8½*, and rubble became the key word. Metaphoric rubble became visual rubble. A theatre is being torn down. On its stage a party in celebration of that. The celebrants for whom the the-atre represents youth, dreams lost, a golden time, are to be orphaned. (Aronson: "There's no place for patina in the United States.") Is the theatre torn down? Will it be torn down tomorrow? Or was it torn down yesterday? Keep it ambiguous, a setting for the sort of introspection that reunions precipitate, a mood in which to lose sight of the present, to look back on the past.

Goldman and Sondheim were about just such business, but not in surrealistic terms. However, they approved of our scheme and agreed to adapt to it.

The title, *Follies,* suggested the *Ziegfeld Follies,* but also, in the British sense, foolishness, and in the French, "folie," which is madness.

Once again Boris went to work, this time creating rubble: a construction of levels, culs de sac, planked paths connected by metal stairways, the whole looking very much like the superstructure from which buildings are torn down. It was cut into three large sections, which were motorized to move upstage and down and diagonally offstage. From the start we had to decide where we would put every scene and number though most were yet to be written.

At this time, naïvely, we figured that Sondheim would be replacing three or four of the numbers in the score. Ultimately, we kept six of the original songs and Steve wrote sixteen new ones.

In the new draft we added four figures of the leading characters as they had existed thirty years earlier. So much ectoplasm, they were to wander as silent memories across the paths of their present selves.

It worked so well that Goldman gave them words to speak. They intruded more and more into the evening, taking stage, confusing time, confronting the present with the past until ultimately in a sort of collective nervous breakdown, they took over.

Bennett suggested dressing them in black and white, and putting clown-white makeup and black lipstick on them. For a time we even considered having them cross into color in the Follies section, with our four leads fading into black and white. In this show everything qualified for consideration, no matter how lunatic.

Bennett wanted a grouping of unearthly plaster mannequin-showgirls in period costumes spanning fifty years to be displayed in the structure and changed during the evening. As the four young characters were given dialogue, he replaced them with living statues, ghostly showgirls wandering slowly and silently through the evening, their costumes and makeup black and white.

Florence Klotz designed two hundred costumes over a period of nine months. It was a monumental job, exquisitely realized.

The show arced to a mini *Ziegfeld Follies,* giving the audience in the final twenty minutes what it had expected all along. The only difference was that the stars of our Follies would confront in lavish production numbers the lies that had led them relentlessly to the brink of madness. Defenseless, they would lay waste the past, leave the rubble of the theatre behind them, and start to live. It was clear what we wanted to do. But how to do it? The rehearsal script was more a screenplay than a stage play, with our equivalents of pans and tracking shots and dissolves. You can even give the effect of a close-up by isolating a person onstage.

We went into rehearsal without the Follies section, seventy pages of script culminating in a Goldman-inspired confrontation of eight people, the four principals and their young counterparts in a Laocoön tangle, screaming at one another on an empty stage and suddenly trapped in a Ziegfeld extravaganza.

The script quit abruptly with these words: "What follows is a capsule Follies—costume parades, comedy routines, specialty acts—traditional and accurate in all ways but one. Sets, costumes, music, movement; all this is faithful to the past. What's different and unusual about it is the content, what it's all about."

This was the last page in our script for the first four weeks of a six-week rehearsal period. I wouldn't take that chance with anyone but Steve Sondheim. It was a maddening experience, particularly for Michael Bennett, as the nonexistent Follies section was his responsibility to stage. Steve filtered material to him the beginning of the fifth week of rehearsal with the Boston opening staring us in the face.

There were to be five numbers. "Loveland," for the entire company, was finished first (in fact, Steve wrote in sequence). Then came a number for each of the young couples ("You're Gonna Love Tomorrow" and "Love Will See Us Through"). Then "Losing My Mind," which had been rejected from the original *Girls Upstairs* but was earmarked for Alexis Smith (PHYLLIS). Numbers were to be written for Dorothy Collins, Gene Nelson, and John McMartin. He was even contemplating one for Yvonne de Carlo, perhaps to be shared with the other supporting ladies.

At one point Alexis, who had learned "Losing My Mind," wisely suggested that the song was dead wrong for her, following as it does "Leave You," her other solo, and giving her no opportunity to move.

We agreed, and for a time it left Steve with four songs to write in ten days.

Now every day's rehearsal—and the days rarely ended before midnight—included an additional hour or two of talk, with and for Steve, about each of the four characters and how best to explain what they had learned during the evening at the party, what insights into their conflict had been revealed. During these sessions, it became clear that BUDDY (Gene Nelson) was a masochist, rejecting love, courting rejection. So Steve wrote "Buddy's Blues" and Michael Bennett staged it.

Dorothy Collins' SALLY learned nothing from the evening. Stripped of her lie, she went mad. Inadvertently Steve had written her song. "Losing My Mind" gave her the chance, in Follies terms, to be Helen Morgan. It worked. Michael's assistant, Bob Avian, staged that number.

Five down and two to go, entering our sixth week of rehearsal. Steve wrote an elegant schizoid number for the two sides of Alexis' character and called it "Uptown, Downtown." He had the right idea and replaced it with a better number, "The Story of Lucy and Jessie," in Boston.

We'd rehearsed the first month at the American Theatre Lab, which is Jerry Robbins' dance studio, on a mockup of the set with indicated elevations—one foot for every five. The final two weeks we moved to the Feller Scenic Studio in the Bronx and worked on the finished set. Aside from the elevations and the staircases, the great maw that we worked in was heavily raked, and it was a shock to our company to see the angle on which they were expected not only to walk, but to tapdance. It saved a great deal of money adjusting there (instead of in Boston with stagehands and orchestra hanging around).

In the middle of the last week we still lacked BEN's (John McMartin) number, which was to include the company. "Live, Laugh, Love" arrived the last day of rehearsal, and while they were dismantling the set and loading the vans for Boston, Hal Hastings, our musical director, taught McMartin the lyric and melody, and Michael Bennett choreographed the dancers. He completed the work in the Bradford Hotel ballroom in Boston and on the set at the Colonial Theatre while the stagehands focused the lights and hung the drops.

Coming out of McMartin's number, we planned a Felliniesque kaleidoscope of impressions of the events of the evening. Jim Goldman improvised a scene, I staged it, ending in chaos, using the fifty members of the company all over the set. Again, in Boston, at dress rehearsal, with Tharon Musser still lighting, the cast in costume, and the orchestra in the pit for the first time, the chaos was choreographed, adapted to the moving scenery, and something achieved acceptable to open with.

When you go to Boston, that's all you really try to do: tie up the loose ends and get the curtain up and down for your first public performance. We usually schedule it for a Saturday, which gives us Sunday without scenery and costumes for cutting and polishing. On Monday afternoon we schedule a full technical rehearsal, and by Monday night the show is beginning to look like something.

In the case of *Follies,* I decided not to open in Boston until the Wednesday, which gave us six full technical rehearsals before getting reviewed.

Michael Bennett had an interesting technique for implementing the ensemble singing during the tapdancing sequences. He recorded the company in rehearsal and had them sing in sync with their own voices in performance; otherwise they would have been too winded to achieve any volume.

Movies have been using the click-track and prerecorded tapes for years.

Ordinarily I abhor this sort of thing. We didn't even use microphones until *West Side Story,* and there were never any problems. But performers aren't trained to project their singing voices and rarely do they know how to protect them. Audiences, meanwhile, aren't trained to listen. The advent of television and electronic instruments has pushed the audience back in its seats. I remember when I first went to theatre, having to adjust for perhaps five minutes to the sounds of the actors. I would sit forward in my seat and the connection that I made with the stage was an investment in the experience. Had I taken away the amplification at *A Little Night Music,* which is a show that could have survived without it, it would have made the audience reach out to the stage. I wish I'd had the courage to do it.

Do we not run the risk of mechanizing the theatre until it becomes so slick it loses its "liveness"? The American musical particularly has for the last fifteen years been overpackaged, overproduced, lacking in content. Content is the key word. Content must always dictate style, form, the use of machinery. As soon as the technical things precede the text, we are in trouble. The salvation of modern theatre rests not with multimedia experiences and hyped-up sound, but the reverse: a return to a less sophisticated, more visceral relationship between actor and audience.

It was characteristic of *Follies* that there was an inordinate number of potential distractions. Gene Nelson was quoted in a magazine interview as saying that the show went against everything he'd been taught about not moving on certain dialogue because the laughs would be lost, about not upstaging key scenes with activity. Throughout *Follies* six-foot showgirls wandered around in incredible costumes, glittering and gleaming upstage of some very serious book scenes, the content of which was necessary to understanding the show. And they were not distracting. It was as though we set our own ground rules and lived by them. The audience knew what to listen to and where to look. We made them work in *Follies,* and some objected. For others, it was exhilarating.

And there was no intermission. *The Girls Upstairs,* without plot or suspense, was to be performed in one act. *Follies* was too long for that, so we lowered the curtain rather arbitrarily halfway into the evening. After the show had found its proper length (two hours and fifteen minutes), we interrupted our show-stopping number ("Who's That Woman?") for the intermission. We brought the curtain down on a stage full of beautiful women tapdancing in unison, raising it for the second act at the same place in the number. It was effective but cut the applause in half.

I'm not concerned with creating show-stoppers. I sometimes think that in the name of perversity (integrity?) I frustrate an audience's desire to applaud, which is contradictory in view of how I feel about involvement.

It took *Follies* five minutes to regain its momentum no matter where we put the intermission. Three days before we opened, Bennett and I were still fighting it out in the lobby. We solved it by playing the show in one act.

The most agonizing time for all of us on *Follies* came when we were in our final week of previews in New York. We had scheduled performances Monday, Tuesday, and Wednesday, with Thursday a day off, and openings on Friday, Saturday, matinee and evening, and Sunday. The critics had been invited to choose which of those four performances they would attend. Tickets had been distributed. On the Monday after the performance, I received a call from Los Angeles telling me that Gene Nelson's son had been hit by a truck on his way home from school and was on the critical list at Cedars of Lebanon Hospital.

I found Gene at home with friends who had seen the preview that night and were quietly celebrating. I got him to a telephone. His wife told him to stay on in New York with the show, that things were encouraging. I spoke separately with Marilyn Nelson, who told me that the child was in a coma and at this point Gene was better off busy working in New York.

The following morning at rehearsal I suggested to the authors and Michael Bennett that we open Wednesday and not run the risk of waiting till the end of the week. Nelson might not be there by then, and even if he were, the pressure of these days would surely affect his performance. Meanwhile, we put his understudy into rehearsal and I called Mary Bryant, our press representative, instructing her to tell the critics what had happened, to swear them to secrecy, and request that they come in that night if possible.

I then called the company together, and reminding them of my abhorrence of openings, announced that I had invited the critics that night. Then I put in a brand-new last scene for John McMartin and Alexis Smith, and McMartin, on whom most of the burden of the new dialogue lay, was letter-perfect.

(Nelson's son remained in a coma for six weeks. The story has a happy ending: he has since recovered completely.)

I made a mistake with the Original Cast album. I neglected to stipulate in the contract with Capitol Records that the entire score be recorded. There were twenty-two songs, and it would have taken four sides. That was not unprecedented. *She Loves Me* had required a double album, and only recently Columbia recorded the whole of *Candide,* dialogue and music. Capitol refused on the grounds that it wouldn't sell. The contracts were signed and there was nothing I could do.

I warned them that there would be many letters of complaint, and there were hundreds. There was more mail for *Follies,* which was never a standing-room-only show, than for *Cabaret,* which was. There were *Follies* "freaks" who saw the show a dozen times or more, and they campaigned in the *Times* for a limited edition of the complete score. But they lost. Cast albums don't sell.

I cannot wait for show scores to come into their own again. It is inevitable. Meantime, the amount of wax (do they still use wax?) wasted on uneducated, lyrically illiterate, popular music is discouraging.

Follies cost $800,000 to produce. It lost $685,000. There were fifty in the cast, thirty in the orchestra, and twenty-eight in the crew backstage. It cost $80,000 a week to break even. At capacity it would have taken approximately forty weeks to pay off. But it wasn't the sort of show that plays to capacity. It ran sixty-five weeks on Broadway with grosses ranging from $113,961 to $31,853. We won seven Tony Awards in April of 1972 and our grosses rose to $91,000 for several weeks, but the summer was coming, so we moved to California and inaugurated the Shubert, the newest theatre in the United States, with a show about tearing down a theatre.

All the reviews were marvelous but the show wasn't popular, and the grosses ranged from $102,376 in the beginning of the run to $55,615 in the final weeks.

I am happy I did *Follies*. I could not do it again because I could not in all conscience raise the money for it. Perhaps it's best summed up by Frank Rich, who was the critic for the *Harvard Crimson* when we were trying out in Boston:

It is easy to avoid *Follies* on the grounds that it is, after all, a Broadway musical—and, given what Broadway musicals have come to mean, such a bias is understandable. But that is precisely why you should see it, for *Follies* is a musical about the death of the musical and everything musicals represented for the people who saw and enjoyed them when such entertainment flourished in this country. If nothing else, *Follies* will make clear to you exactly why such a strange kind of theatre was such an important part of the American consciousness for so long. In the playbill for this show, the setting is described as "a party on the stage of this theatre tonight." They are not kidding, and there is no getting around the fact that a large part of the chilling fascination of *Follies* is that its creators are in essence presenting their own funeral.

He titled his review "The Last Musical." An unanticipated metaphor.

CHAPTER 24

In 1957, right after *West Side Story* opened, Sondheim and I talked about doing a kind of court masque, a chamber opera, elegant, probably about sex, a gavotte in which couples interchange, suffering mightily in elegant country homes, wearing elegant clothes.

We hit upon the idea of adapting Jean Anouilh's *Ring Round the Moon*, and I contacted Jan Van Loewen, Anouilh's agent in London. Steve was not yet known as a composer, and I was solely a producer. Van Loewen informed us that Lerner and Loewe had inquired about the rights (Lord knows why they wanted it after *My Fair Lady*), as had Irene Selznick and Leland Hayward. So we shouldn't hold out much hope.

However, I offered to go to Paris to meet with Anouilh, and was told to come ahead and an appointment was arranged. When I arrived in Paris, Anouilh had left that morning for his home in Switzerland. I'm not that kind of tenacious. Put down by his rudeness, I returned to New York, and we dropped the project.

Probably we were fortunate. I am convinced that in 1958, which was in the eye of the brash, brassy, give-'em-a-lot-of-whoop-up-noise musical, ours would have failed even if the reviews had been good. That's what contributed, I think, to *She Loves Me*'s failure.

The years that followed surfeited that appetite in people, and by 1973, *A Little Night Music* was a blessed relief.

In 1972, after *Follies,* I thought now was the time to do that chamber opera we'd talked about. Again we inquired about *Ring Round the Moon*. Van Loewen wrote back that the author was still reluctant to have it turned into a musical. Would we take *Thieves Carnival* instead? I said no.

I asked Hugh Wheeler to join us. We talked endlessly about various source material, finally singling out Jean Renoir's *Rules of the Game* and Ingmar Bergman's *Smiles of a Summer Night*. We arranged a screening of both films and read both screenplays.

There are interesting similarities in *Rules of the Game, Smiles of a Summer Night,* and *Ring Round the Moon*. Each takes place in a summerhouse on a weekend. Each contains a party, each a play within a play. The characters are similar. There is the old lady in the wheelchair who is adjusted to death. There are the young people on the threshold of life. And there are the lovers in varying degrees of frustration.

I consider us very lucky that Van Loewen and Anouilh turned us down. *Ring Round the Moon* is a much colder piece than *Smiles of a Summer Night*. The characters in it are bloodless, more literary, less dimensional, less involving.

Rules of the Game was a disappointment to all of us, perhaps because it is a classic and so much has been written and said about it.

Smiles of a Summer Night had everything. It had darkness and humanity. It is constructed brilliantly. Bergman wrote the screenplay, and I consider Bergman the writer every bit the measure of Bergman the director.

We contacted him through his lawyer in Sweden. In less than a week we received a wire, asking for further details. Hugh Wheeler wrote a one-page analysis in musical terms and I a covering letter. The purpose was to assure him that we did not intend a literal translation of his screenplay. It was to be "suggested by" rather than "adapted from." Apparently this appealed to him because, again, in less than a week we received a wire giving us the go-ahead, wishing us luck, and asking us to contact his representative, Paul Kohner, in California.

Kohner, over the phone, "My client doesn't like a lot of complicated negotiations. Will you make an offer you consider fair?" I recommended the Christopher Isherwood (*Cabaret*), Nikos Kazantzakis (*Zorba*) royalty arrangement, and it was accepted immediately over the telephone, which is extraordinary, and we went to work.

Some justice: I received a letter from Van Loewen when I arrived in Boston for the tryout of *Night Music,* saying that Anouilh had reconsidered and *Ring Round the Moon* was now available. I had the pleasure of answering that we were about to open *that* show in Boston and obviously I was no longer interested.

Our initial plan was to tell the story of a group of diverse people converging for a weekend in the country. The first act was to introduce the characters and many subplots and was to end with their arrival at an elegant country house. In the second, we were to see three different solutions to the tangled relationships. One melodramatic, the second farcical, and the third (the real one) consistent with the style of the first act.

A Little Night Music suggested a Magritte painting to me. Figures . . . anomalies in a landscape. A gentle greensward on which to play scenes in bedrooms, dressing rooms, dining rooms. I wanted the figures in the landscape out of context, for no more reason than Magritte puts them there.

Steve talked of waltzes. The entire score in three-quarter time. And in some ingenious musical way that I don't understand, everything is indeed in some form of triple time, though not all are waltzes. *Night Music* contains scherzos, minuets, polonaises, barcaroles, and a variety of waltzes.

We wanted to do a kind of Chekovian musical, realizing that would mean considerable exposition in the beginning, moving slowly, no big opening number, but we hoped, in time, we would draw our audience into it.

Early on, Steve asked me to substitute a Liebeslieder Group for a conventional chorus. I asked him how they were to function. He replied that was my problem. He needed them musically. As far as he was concerned, we could put a piano to the side of the stage and they could stand around it as in Balanchine's *Liebeslieder Walzer*. I was in trouble for three months. Meantime, he wrote the score to include them everywhere.

Then I got the idea that they might represent the positive spirits in a negative household. Everyone in *Night Music* is frustrated, humiliated by sexual role-playing. The five Liebeslieder people are secure. Perhaps they are operetta singers, optimistic, extroverted observers. Each is a personality, each has a response to the events of the evening. No two are alike. They make the piece accessible because they lead the audience into it.

One week before we went into rehearsal Equity ruled that the Liebeslieder roles were chorus because they had only songs to sing, solos, mind you, but no dialogue. It threatened to make them sign chorus contracts.

It had been as difficult to cast those five Liebeslieder roles as any in the show. They required not only operatic voices, but presence and acting experience *because* they had no lines in which to develop character. I know we could not have found acceptable replacements for them from the chorus rolls, and they refused to sign chorus contracts. So Equity was threatening the future of the show.

I refused to acquiesce. The artists and I decided instead to go ahead with rehearsals despite daily harassment from the union and face arbitration proceedings. Equity backed down. When it came time to cast the national company, they tried to enforce it all over again. And failed.

If Actors' Equity insists on shackling the creators of shows, if it legislates the hiring of either less experienced or less talented personnel for roles which I consider as individual and responsible as any of the roles in a play, it will discourage employment because I will not make these compromises.

It occurs to me each time I come to a showdown with the unions that my position is backed up by twenty years of producing. I have some clout. No wonder there are so few new producers.

When *Night Music* was in Boston, Sondheim came to me concerned that too many people felt the show was slow starting and couldn't we do something about it. I reminded him that we had set out to do a Chekovian musical, that there was no way to be true to our objectives and satisfy the conventional demands of some of our audience.

Over the years I have grown to know how little Sondheim concerns himself with popular tastes, how obstinately he eschews the familiar solution. So this was a unique request. The only thing we did consciously to relax our audience was introduce the Liebeslieder Group at the top of the evening to perform the overture. It suggested a musical was to follow without affecting the introduction of the characters and early exposition, which were nonmusical.

Boris Aronson was reluctant to design *Night Music*. He kept reminding me that he is a Russian. I said I didn't know the difference between the landscape in Leningrad and the landscape in Helsinki: it's all birch trees as far as I am concerned. So he painted a forest of birch trees on clear plastic to look like Fabergé enamel on crystal. He carpeted the stage in a gently rolling green lawn. Again, the scenery was designed before the show was written, just as in *Follies* and *Company*.

His first designs included sections of wall, real doors, and chandeliers encompassed in the woods. Quickly, I eliminated these, reducing the production to choice pieces of antique furniture isolated among the trees. That made Boris nervous up until rehearsals. Over the summer, without my knowledge, he designed a totally new scheme, which he showed me when I came back in September. I didn't care for it and we went right back to the original designs.

The next problem was Hugh Wheeler's. Our extravagant plotting of the second act plus Boris' plans (involving beds on lawns in front of the houses they were supposed to be inside of!) inhibited him, and he couldn't write. The first draft was a big disappointment.

I suggested that he forget everything we'd talked about conceptually, that he write his play (not ours), better still, a screenplay, and forget it was to be a musical. Within two weeks he turned in a finished script.

Hugh Wheeler (*Big Fish, Little Fish* deserves a new production. I believe today it would succeed) is one of the few serious playwrights who can handle the stresses of musical collaboration. His peers shy away from writing libretti on the basis that the composer and director get all the credit. Hugh's experience with *Night Music* and later *Candide* surely has given the lie to that.

The last fifteen minutes of *Night Music* take place in a country house. There are long hallways and much of the stage business has to do with doors opening and closing. I took a bed from Désirée's bedroom, a wicker armchair from her mother's sitting room, a bench from the corner of the park, a statue of cupid at the entrance to a gazebo, an alcove in a child's room, and put them at once on the lawn in front of the country house. The audience supplied the hallways and the doors. Hugh Wheeler didn't have to rewrite a word.

I have always found Scandinavian theatre engrossing,

but a little alien. I understand Nora's slamming that door, but I have a hell of a lot of trouble empathizing on the way there.

Ingmar Bergman's work is always fascinating but often it keeps me at arm's length. I am in the company of exotic strangers.

My wife and I observed that first hand a year before I did *Night Music.* Sweden is primeval territory. The reactions of individuals are curious, unfamiliar, what causes them to laugh, what engages them. Perhaps it is the light, adjusting to unnaturally long days and endless nights, that does eerie things to their psyches. "Perpetual sunset is rather an unsettling thing. . . ."

Steve immediately responded to the darker side, but Hugh and I felt uncomfortable with this tone in Bergman's material.

Bergman came to see the show in November 1973. Generous in his approval, he did say, ". . . I was surprised that it was possible to eliminate the shadows of desperation, eroticism, and caprice without the whole story collapsing. At the moment I forgot that this entertaining and witty musical had anything to do with my picture. I enjoyed it tremendously and I loved your actors. . . ."

Pat Birch agreed to choreograph although there were no dancers in the show and little opportunity for dances as such. But dances don't interest her half so much as character and movement and the total musical. *Night Music* tried to be seamless, and when we collaborate, it's difficult to know where she leaves off and I start.

With the show ready to go into rehearsal, Steve had completed only half the score. The balance came in slowly, but the actors were patient. Glynis Johns's "Send in the Clowns" arrived two days before we left for Boston.

I staged the book, and with Pat, Steve's eight numbers, in the first two weeks, and there was nothing to do but await the rest, while fussing with what we had, which is dangerous because you are still too close to it.

The final scene in Act I was a sequence for the entire company, to be musicalized, a miniopera. I got tired of waiting, and one day with some ad libs from Hugh I began to move the actors around:

You go here and you hand this person an invitation and you say, "Look what happened, We've been invited to a weekend at the Armfeldts' in the country," and you say, "Well, I don't want to go," and you say, "Oh, please," and you say, "Well, I'll reconsider," and so on.

I took the company through these little scenes, perhaps six of them. Each time I came to the end of one, I would say, "Now you sing" or "You two sing" or "All four of you sing." And catching the spirit, with vocalizing and appropriate gestures, they made a mock opera of it. Simultaneously I choreographed the birch trees to go with the scene changes and dialogue.

I invited Steve to see what we'd done and he went home that night and wrote a fifteen-minute sequence so specifically that Pat Birch was able to choreograph the company without altering the blocking. "A Weekend in the Country" is such an accomplishment that Steve was prompted to suggest that next time we should stage our libretto without any music, show it to him, then let him go away for six months to write the score.

I had trouble raising money for *Night Music,* primarily because of *Follies.* Many of my investors counted on the return from a previous show to finance their next investment, so we were able to raise only a little more than half of what we needed. I was surprised.

I had no right to be surprised. I had always believed it one of Broadway's virtues that you can't ride on past successes. Nevertheless, I was upset. I was affronted! I raised the money, but it was difficult, and we were in rehearsal a week before we were capitalized.

I felt the pressure from rehearsals through the opening in New York. If this one didn't pay off, I would be back doing auditions. In 1953, when we hustled for the *Pajama Game* money, it was fun. I was a kid and it was all part of the game. It doesn't represent fun to me any more. All that Frank Merriwell stuff is behind me.

I am constantly brought up short by the necessity of appearing a businessman in order to do what I want to do. There's nothing onerous about being a businessman; it's simply unfair that that should be a requirement for artistic continuity.

In addition, I spent the Boston opening worrying about capital running out, whether the reviews would be good enough to help us meet operating expenses, how much would be left in the event we couldn't. There's a sinking fund of $35,000 in each show. It has been that figure for twenty years; $35,000 doesn't last long if you're in trouble.

Additionally depressing: This time the record companies weren't anxious to audition the score. Columbia Records had put a great deal of money into the *Dude* recording, and only out of respect for Sondheim and my office agreed to hear *A Little Night Music*. Clive Davis, who has since left Columbia, sat distractedly checking his fingernails for the better part of forty minutes while I told the story and Sondheim played the music. A day or so later Tom Shepard, then a producer of records at Columbia, phoned me to say that they were going to "pass on this one," that it was his feeling that though the work we were doing was beautiful, we were in fact "casting pearls before swine." Did he mean his compatriots or the theatregoing public?

Subsequently, Goddard Lieberson, who had semiretired from Columbia Records, came to see a preview in New York. At his insistence Columbia negotiated for the recording.

In the interim we played the score for RCA, with whom I had done *Fiddler on the Roof*. Fourteen executives arranged themselves in a studio on Sixth Avenue. Sondheim and I were five minutes into our audition when a secretary came in and appropriated one of the executives for a telephone conference. Soon another secretary came in with advertising copy for approval, a third with some letters to sign. There was steady traffic of executives and their secretaries, a hum in the background of phone conversations. In forty minutes, when we were finished, of the original fourteen people, only five remained.

I am told the *Night Music* cast album is the first non-rock theatre score to have paid back its expenses in many years. Encouraging.

We were a week away from the New York opening when Glynis Johns fell ill. She has a history of hypoglycemia, and she had been fading fast, until one night, three days before our opening, she collapsed and was taken to the hospital.

We put her understudy, Barbara Lang, on in the role and because there had been so much excitement about the show, people kept their seats and Barbara did well. She's young for Désirée, and she's close to five feet ten, so the costumes, which had trailed on the floor for Glynis, were a few inches off it for Barbara.

That evening I postponed the opening indefinitely. It was too soon to know what shape Glynis was in, and we had thought of only one possible replacement—Tammy Grimes. She came to see it and we talked about getting her up in the part and opening a week late. She agreed, but she also raised a number of questions respecting interpretation, attitudes, and, most specifically, the costumes. It was too late to make the kind of changes she was suggesting. For the show to open with a substitute star in seven days it would have to be the one I had rehearsed, and any alterations, including to the costumes, would have to be just that—alterations.

I stayed up most of the night worrying and decided to continue the previews indefinitely while I flew to London to seek a replacement. The following morning I went to see Glynis in the hospital. She looked marvelous.

I contacted the newspapers to say that we would be opening as originally scheduled. Glynis was back on the stage the following evening, and we opened the day after that.

The reviews were excellent. Clive Barnes called it an opera in his opening paragraph. I always thought operas closed on Saturday night. So much for rules.

I do not see the natural progression from *Company* to *Follies* to *Night Music* that some critics pointed out in their reviews, and I take perverse pleasure in the fact that *Night Music* has enough plot for two musicals and followed *Follies,* which had encouraged the critics to predict that we were moving inexorably in the direction of the plotless musical.

I didn't enjoy doing *A Little Night Music.* I suffered no sleepless nights. I wasn't digging deep into myself. Of course, there are things I learned: the dinner-table scene, of which I'm very proud, and the final scene, on the lawn, are extensions of techniques begun with *Cabaret* and better realized with the birthday parties in *Company.*

But mostly *Night Music* was about having a hit.

CHAPTER 25

T. Edward Hambleton invited me to join the board of
the Phoenix about fifteen years ago. I don't quite know
what he expected of me, but he's a very tenacious fellow
and maybe he expected that some day I would turn into
a director and want to direct plays for them.

In 1961 he asked me to direct a production of *The
Matchmaker,* which was being financed by the New York
State Arts Council and produced by the Phoenix. It would
star Sylvia Sidney and would tour New York State, opening in the theatre at Vassar College. It was a first offer
professionally for me, and I accepted.

I remained on the board during the golden days of the
APA-Phoenix collaboration. When the APA departed, the
Phoenix went through a period of treading water. There
was a good production that Stephen Porter directed of
Harvey with Helen Hayes and Jimmy Stewart, one year
later *The Catonsville Nine* and *School for Wives,* both
first rate, and the year after an unsuccessful *Murderous
Angels.*

But that's not the point; the point is I couldn't define a credo for the Phoenix, and I said as much at a board meeting.

Once again the Phoenix redefined its objectives. I was asked to become an artistic director along with Stephen Porter, and since neither of us had the time and inclination for administration, we invited Michael Montel, who had been casting director for the Mark Taper Forum in Los Angeles and had directed there, to join us. He would reestablish the Side Show Program, producing five or six plays-in-progress while Porter and I directed one play each.

The New Phoenix Repertory Company would open in Philadelphia at the Annenberg Center on the campus of the University of Pennsylvania and would tour college cities. In Philadelphia, Boston, and New York consortiums of universities and colleges would be created to build up subscription audiences. We would play one-nighters and split weeks in smaller college towns: Ann Arbor (University of Michigan), Storrs (University of Connecticut), Bloomington (Indiana University), and Princeton. New York would simply be another stop in the tour.

From the point of view of the National Endowment and the larger foundations, we would be supplying productions of classics of high quality, performed in repertory, and there is no other company in the United States doing that today.

I chose O'Neill's *The Great God Brown* and Porter chose Molière's *Don Juan* for the first season (1972–73). Our reviews were better than the size of our audiences and every week was a losing week.

The second season (1973–74) I directed Duerrenmatt's

The Visit, Porter did *Chemin de Fer,* and we added a third play, Philip Barry's *Holiday,* directed by Montel.

I chose *The Great God Brown* because I'd read it in college and I wondered how it worked. It is flawed and over-written, but it is passionate. It is a much better play than I thought when I began directing it. Only in rehearsal did I realize how adroitly constructed it is, how motivated the characters. I think it is a clear and brilliant play but must acknowledge its inaccessibility to others.

The Visit is another matter. Also a well-made play, it is not an embarrassing play. It is depressing but curiously exhilarating. It can be done realistically, surrealistically, or expressionistically. I chose the last.

I visited Duerrenmatt in Switzerland. During the interview in which I spoke French and he replied in German, he encouraged me to direct a more audacious—if that's the word—primitive, vulgar—that *is* the word—version of the play. He said he had recently seen the opera at Glynde-bourne, and it was heavy and dark, and he liked that.

I had seen the Lunts in *The Visit,* and they were very grand, very adept, very glamorous. But I didn't remember the play or the other people in it. The original produc-tion, which Peter Brook directed, had about forty-five in the cast. The Phoenix can afford but eighteen.

I asked Ed Burbridge, the designer, for three flat panels, maybe eight feet high and five feet across, to be used throughout the evening. Made of shiny vinyl, in the first act they would be black, in the second blood red, and in the third white. These panels would be moved around the stage by the actors to represent trees, to enclose a room, to make a path.

Burbridge surprised me with three periactoids, triangular-shaped units, eight feet tall, three feet six inches across, on casters, that could be turned easily by any one member of the company. He added a circular iron staircase on top of which was a black tufted-leather banquette, the balcony of the Golden Apostle Inn. And he designed a drop with the name of the town, Gullen, made of bits of broken glass. The triangles were covered in wood, glass, and ceramic for the first two acts, and in the third act, mirror.

The production was so spare I used Clara Zachanassian's baggage to serve as furniture.

I had never seen a Bauhaus theatre production, but the Phoenix budget encouraged such a concept, and it produced unexpected advantages. The Brook production had eliminated certain sequences because they were too cumbersome. One, in particular, an automobile ride through the village and surrounding forest, became my favorite scene in the play. Seated on a pile of luggage, Schill and his family were propelled around the stage on a baggage cart through a forest of slowly turning mirrored triangles.

There's a great deal of talk about the loss of an audience for serious theatre on Broadway. That was true in the 1950s and 1960s, when the Broadway audience represented a narrow spectrum of the public, when it opted exclusively for musicals and situation comedies. In those years the less affluent, more intellectual audience visited Off-Broadway and Off-Off-Broadway, and the young audience was addicted to film.

By the 1960s the regional theatre was flourishing. Actors, directors, designers were getting the sort of theatrical training that had been denied them for more than thirty-five years. And young people discovered the theatre in the regions.

Predictably, during that period, competitive lines were drawn, separating Broadway from "the theatre." The important press had a great deal to do with promulgating that.

During the 1970s, perhaps we will come to accept the obvious: we're all in it together.

The run of a serious play today is no more a gauge of its success than ever. Shakespeare doesn't play a thousand performances. O'Neill didn't. The only difference between 1973 and 1923 is economics. Take a look at these performance figures of plays which have entered the rolls of permanent theatre literature.

A Moon for the Misbegotten	68
Amphitryon 38	153
Anna Christie	177
The Circle	175
The Crucible	197
Ethan Frome	120
Design For Living	135
The Iceman Cometh	136
Winterset	195
Outward Bound	144
The Time of Your Life	185
The Petrified Forest	197

The serious play today has to be subsidized by the foundations and presented by a nonprofit organization.

(Ironically, I wrote the above before *A Moon for the*

Misbegotten became the most successful play on Broadway during the season of 1974. It is commercially presented and represents a windfall for its investors. At this writing, it has played 225 performances at capacity.)

In its second season the New Phoenix Repertory Company increased its audience in Philadelphia by 25 per cent, in Boston by a third, and in New York by 400 per cent.

Doesn't it follow that whatever the public wants, the commercial producer supplies? That's not the best thing you can say about us, but it is a fact.

CHAPTER 26

I first heard of the Chelsea about ten years ago when Anthony Perkins asked me to lend my name to the Advisory Board for a new theatre group working out of a church in the Chelsea area of New York. I agreed, and forgot about it.

Years later I was in Brooklyn to see the Chelsea Theatre Center's impressive production of Edward Bond's *Saved*. After the performance Bob Kalfin, the artistic director of the company, introduced himself to me and pointed out that I was a member of their Advisory Board. Subsequently, I made a number of return visits to the Chelsea and the work was always superior.

Kalfin called me one day to ask whether I would be interested in working with them, and I said I would indeed. He suggested a revival of the Bernstein-Hellman-Wilbur-Latouche-Voltaire *Candide,* which had been done in 1956 on Broadway.

I told him I didn't think a revival would work. I had seen the original and it was ponderous and a bore, and

I remembered it well. The score was exciting, but the performance confusing. I tend to think the production failed at the top from that confusion. Half the show was politically and socially oriented and the other half was oriented to the satirization of musical operetta, Bernstein's musical-theatre joke.

I think it's unfair to say, as some people have, that the book was the villain. Tyrone Guthrie takes second place to no one in recent theatre history, but he made his mistakes and *Candide* was one of them. The book, music, lyrics, and physical production were inappropriate to one another.

About six months later Kalfin called again and said he had a young man working on it, reshaping Hellman's original material. I read it, didn't think it accomplished much, and forgot about *Candide* again.

Three months later *Night Music* was open, and I was looking for something to do for the 1973–74 season. Obviously, I couldn't get a new musical ready, and I began to think about *Candide*.

The first thing I did was read Voltaire. I had never read *Candide*. I was surprised by how light and impulsive and irreverant and *unimportant* it is. Apparently he wrote it quickly and denied having written it, putting it down as a schoolboy's prank. And that's the spirit of it.

The three hundred and some odd years that separated Voltaire's writing it and the Guthrie version of it had served only to make a classic of it and spoil the fun.

Our version would have to be as outrageous in contemporary terms and, curiously, as naïve.

I started to think about the structure of it, and the

problem that telling a picaresque story with an infinite number of highs and lows and no real crises presents in the theatre.

It becomes boring. The hero beginning his odyssey, runs into negative forces and overcomes them or subverts them, and then runs into more negative forces and more negative forces, and then after a while, a pattern is achieved and the audience loses interest.

Therefore, it must be a short evening. Anything that followed an intermission would seem to reprise the first act. Arbitrarily, I decided an hour and forty-five minutes was the proper length for the show. And when it went into rehearsal, it ran an hour and forty-five minutes. (Today it runs an hour and fifty-seven minutes—with laughs.)

I have talked about using a painting, a piece of sculpture, something visual to synthesize a play for me. What was *Candide*? A cartoon, of course, but that came later. More specifically, how to illustrate a picaresque story in static terms? A triptych. But how do you animate a triptych?

I thought immediately of a sideshow at the circus, a series of elevated platforms, in one, the Fat Lady, in others the Sword Swallower, the Tattooed Man, the Bearded Woman, the Siamese Twins, and so on.

Supposing you were guided by the barker (Voltaire?) on foot from one booth to the other along the route of Candide's odyssey. The booths would have little curtains and behind one there would be Lisbon in the throes of a child's-eye version of an earthquake. Another booth would contain war, another a gambling casino in Venice. The booths would be of different sizes, as they are in the circus, and the painting would be primitive, garish, indicating events, leaving the better part of detail to the imagination; the less specific, the more participation from the by-standers.

Once I had gone that far, I realized even *it* was sche-matic and would defeat an hour-and-forty-five-minute piece.

Nevertheless, some version of it would work.

I called Kalfin and told him what was on my mind. He liked it. I suggested we approach Lillian Hellman and ask her whether she would be willing to write a new *Candide*. I told her our scheme and she said that was what she had always wanted, but *Candide*? Never again! In that case, would she object to my asking someone else to work with me? Immediately, she agreed. (When subsequently I put it to Bernstein and Wilbur and they agreed, I figured all of them wanted to lay *Candide* to rest once and for all.) The only proviso she made was that none of her original dialogue be retained in the new version.

I then called Hugh Wheeler. We met and listened to the album. Each of us took the Voltaire and underlined choice bits, going over what particularly delighted us. He went away to write it *before* the lawyers and agents had met and contracts had been negotiated.

That was a complicated business from the Chelsea's point of view because the original not only had Bernstein as composer and Hellman as author, but Wilbur, La-touche, Hellman, Bernstein, and Dorothy Parker as lyri-cists.

Hugh and I paid Bernstein a visit and told him our plan (he said it was what he had always wanted) and discussed new numbers—in particular an opening. I did not want to open with "The Best of All Possible Worlds" because it is a statement of philosophy, the idea rather than an introduction of the characters, the emotion. The original version was cerebral, keeping the audience at arm's length. Ours must be visceral, must envelop the audience.

Once again we had a show that needed an opening number to tell the audience who its main characters are and set the style.

Next, Hugh rejected Venice, rejected Paris (and along with them, some of our favorite numbers, "What's the Use?" and "The Paris Mazurka." Ultimately, we did use the theme of "The Mazurka," but the show never visited Paris). We were going to use episodes from Voltaire that hadn't taken place in the original musical—Constantinople for one.

Bernstein produced a file of melodies, themes, full songs in some instances, of discarded material from 1955–56. There was enough musical material to accommodate the new version, but who was to write the new lyrics? Lenny had, in fact, written "I Am Easily Assimilated" in its entirety, and the "Auto da Fé" with John Latouche, which though discarded in 1956 became valuable to us. But he was scheduled for a series of lectures at Harvard. Given the short time we had to work, it seemed expeditious to ask Steve Sondheim to help us out since I had never met Richard Wilbur.

Wheeler finished a first draft in two weeks. Although not the rehearsal version, it was hilarious.

Chelsea arranged interviews with designers, among them

Eugene Lee. I had seen his environmental set for LeRoi Jones's *Slave Ship* at the Chelsea some seasons earlier. More recently, he had been working with Peter Brook. I went through the whole trajectory of my thinking process, arriving at the sideshow scheme, voicing concern about the schematicness of it. Immediately he suggested limiting curtains to some stages and varying the levels as well as the sizes of them. This suggested to me the possibility of playing scenes simultaneously on stages in opposite ends of the theatre. For the first time I remembered the extraordinary Italian production of *Orlando Furioso,* which I had seen in Bryant Park in 1970 and which clearly hovered somewhere in my subconscious.

I had a thought about "Glitter and Be Gay," Cunégonde's aria: there would be a pianist, the real thing, in eighteenth-century French dress, white-powdered wig, big bosom with beauty mark, her wig emblazoned with diamonds, appearing from a sort of trapdoor concealed in one of the stages. (Lee loved that.) During the song Cunégonde would denude the powdered wig of its diamonds, covering herself with them.

So a trapdoor had entered the conversation and we began breaking the sideshow pattern. Had I any objections to people *sitting* in places other than the center of the environment? Sitting? Well, you can hardly expect them to stand for two hours. Hardly. I had no objection. How about all over the set? Did I object to that? No objection.

Lee and his wife, Franne, live on a sailboat off Providence, Rhode Island, and he went home to work. In about a month he was back with drawings, elevations. I told him I can't read drawings, he would have to construct a model for me. He returned with a shoebox, inside which was a model for *Candide* as it would look in the Chelsea.

We were going to use a ballroom at the Brooklyn Academy of Music that Harvey Lichtenstein had converted into a theatre. It would have held 500 people. It was long and narrow, high ceilinged, and had a balcony about fifteen to eighteen feet up. Most of the thinking I did was based on that room. Soon after I learned that Peter Brook had preempted it and we were switching to the Chelsea's regular theatre, which seats 180 people.

At this point Pat Birch asked me what my plans were for the following season. I told her about Brooklyn and that I assumed with all her offers to choreograph on Broadway (it seemed to me she'd been offered everything the following season), she wouldn't be interested. On the contrary, Brooklyn was going to be fun, and she wanted to be there.

From mid-April I started to walk around with my shoebox. I took my shoebox to Europe, I looked at my shoebox on the mantelpiece in Spain all summer, and I returned to New York in the fall with my shoebox.

As rehearsals approached, Lee asked me what my adjustment to the shoe box was. Did I think of it as a small one or a big one? I realized that I was looking at it and seeing the Broadhurst Theatre, and he was looking at it and seeing the Chelsea, fourth floor of the Brooklyn Academy. I am jumping ahead, but in September, when I went to Brooklyn to see the space without seats in it, I went into shock.

Later when we decided to bring *Candide* to Broadway, I had no worries about the adjustment from the Chelsea to the Broadway Theatre. If there was one thing that bothered me about the production in Brooklyn, it was that there were too few people watching it. The relationship of the people with the people, the audience with the audience, is what makes *Candide* exceptional. The relationship of audience with actor is fairly standard.

People are self-conscious about responding when they're alone, and 180 people in the Chelsea were, except in a few areas, very much alone. If they wanted to laugh, they were aware that they might just be laughing by themselves. In Brooklyn we found that sometimes we had celebrations with our audiences, but more often we had silence. Smiling, grinning, nudging each other, but self-consciously editing audibility out of their responses.

Of course, there's a certain amount of the Richard Schechner Performing Garage business of people coming near you and touching you, but that's kept to a minimum.

I have my own problems with this. As a member of the audience I don't really enjoy actors mauling me, kissing me, hugging me, or grabbing me.

I remember that when I saw *The Blacks* at the Negro Ensemble Company, I was sitting in the front row, and they put a crown in my lap. Later on, Roscoe Lee Browne ordered me to bring the crown back to the center of the stage. I was appalled that I had to rise and move into the play. The response at least was intended.

Not so when I went to see Grotowski. I was hit in the leg with a loaf of bread. That did little to draw me into the experience. More predictably, it alienated me.

So in the case of *Candide,* I instructed the actors, who are never more than a foot away from some of the audience, to be extremely polite, mindful of their intrusion on the audience's privacy. I instructed them to say "Please" when they wanted something and "Excuse me" and "Pardon me" when they were crossing in front of someone. That "Excuse me" was mentioned in almost every review.

The original shoebox contained seven playing areas and during the course of the next six months, before we went into rehearsal, we shuffled those areas, particularly the entrances and exits, the number of trapdoors, stairways; but the final set retained seven stages, two of which are proscenium, a connecting ramp, and two bridges.

Bernstein suggested we reorchestrate the show for everything from one to thirteen instruments, with the emphasis on smaller groups. Obviously, I left all that to him and Hershy Kay, who had originally orchestrated *Candide* and was eager to do a totally different shoestring version of it, and the musical director, John Mauceri.

Mauceri, regular conductor of the Yale Symphony, had conducted Bernstein's *Mass* in Vienna. He was in the process of signing as an assistant to Pierre Boulez at the New York Philharmonic.

So Bernstein, Kay, and Mauceri designed what has now been called a quadraphonic concept, simply: thirteen musicians parceled out in four separate areas of the theatre and surrounding the audience.

I wanted, before I left for my summer in Europe, to have the costume designs in work and a certain amount of casting done. Eugene Lee introduced me to his wife, who had designed the André Gregory *Alice in Wonderland*. Ours was an eccentric encounter.

She brought me a tattered black leather valise in which

she had crammed bits of fabric, remnants from old costumes, old clothes, a piece of a shawl, an antimacasser from the back of a Victorian chair, a codpiece, a comb, a flower, a swatch of mattress ticking. Everything in the show would be made out of something used (later, when I had a series of run-throughs, one friend spotted it: "You can't get those 'whites' in less than fifty years of washing."), and that would give it the feeling that we had emptied a closet, unlocked an attic trunk, a multiplicity of events, times, places.

She put three or four of these pieces on my desk and told me that they looked like the character of the Old Lady. Another collage, Cunégonde. If I put one next to another, against a third, I began to see the characters emerging. Something meshed, something seemed right about that kind of thinking. Now that I've seen how she executes her rather primitive sketches, I am surprised how sophisticated and detailed the work is. And witty.

Had I been doing a show for $600,000, I wouldn't have had the guts to go along with it. And therein lies one of the problems of the commercial theatre.

With *Candide* the risks were all artistic, and artistic risks must always be taken. You need never characterize whether you can afford them or not. The trouble too often in the commercial theatre is that artistic risks are disproportionately magnified.

There were to be six principal characters and six young men and six young girls, all of whom danced and sang, to play the rest of the roles.

Hugh and I decided early, before the first writing of the script, that whereas in the original production Pangloss had played one additional character, in our version, aside from Voltaire, he must appear as a major character in every sequence.

I talked to Jerry Orbach, not only a good friend, but an adept farceur, about playing Voltaire/Pangloss. He was interested, and I let it go at that.

The next most important parts to cast were Candide and Cunégonde. In 1956 they had been trapped by the requirements of the score into being legitimate opera singers, and excepting Barbara Cook, were too old for their roles. It was characterstic of that production that the performers seemed to watch from outside themselves and comment on the text.

We must have children this time, or as close as we could come to them. Our casting call at the Chelsea was for actors between the ages of sixteen and twenty. (Eventually we decided to look for our musicians from the rolls of newly graduated Juilliard students. On Broadway even our ushers are young.)

I don't know how many Cunégondes we saw. An awful lot of girls can sing the "jewel song," but almost all of them kid the character. It seems irresistible to satirize Cunégonde.

Mark Baker and Maureen Brennan auditioned early on. They read beautifully, but the music department raised objections. So instead of signing Maureen and Mark in May, I agreed that the Chelsea and the music department would continue to look during the summer for other people, that Maureen and Mark would work on the score, and, come Labor Day, we would make a decision.

Meantime, I asked Nancy Walker to play the Old Lady

(she wasn't interested) and Julie Newmar to play Paquette, the maid (she was).

Hugh was to arrive in the middle of the summer, which meant that I had about six weeks to forget the project. I had the designs and a script, the original *Candide* recording—I could play it occasionally when I felt like it— but I didn't have to concentrate, I didn't have any deadlines to meet. So I accepted and rejected the imminence of it as the spirit moved me. If I was a little bit bored and sunlogged, I began to think of *Candide* and ideas came. Simple ideas: perhaps the notion that the two kids undress each other during the song "Oh, Happy We," playing against the materialism in the lyrics.

My scripts are a mess by the first day of rehearsal. Covered in squiggles, they document better than anything the changes in tone and detail that inform a project. Not only do I note specific staging ideas, but characteristics that I think are quirky or perverse, inconsistent. I'll write down Gertrude Stein's observation, "When you get there, there's no there there," and what caused me to think of it. Perhaps I'll see someone in a restaurant and I'll draw a picture of the hat she wore or tear out an illustration from a magazine. Collecting things on the way to rehearsal, and more and more striking them out with a red pencil, or writing "No!" meaning awful idea, inconsistent, or no longer valid. I don't have the self-discipline to cram for a play, cram atmosphere, cram character, delve microscopically into each speech to see what the subtext is. Instead, I take my time, and everything collects inside, where I can call on it instinctively.

At one point in the summer Jerry Orbach wrote, saying

he had been offered the lead in *Mack and Mabel*, a David Merrick musical, and if by any chance *Candide* should extend its run in Brooklyn, he would not be available.

So Orbach was out. At the suggestion of friends at the Mark Taper, I asked Roscoe Lee Browne whether he would be interested. His agent in New York turned it down. And then I thought of Lewis Stadlen, who had been brilliant as Groucho Marx in *Minnie's Boys*. We made him an offer, but that remained unresolved until the fall.

Because I couldn't think of anybody to replace Nancy Walker and because Lewis Stadlen is in his twenties, I thought we should be consistent and cast young. Which made a problem with Julie Newmar.

We signed Mark Baker and Maureen Brennan. Then Lewis Stadlen turned us down on the basis that a stage direction in the script said "Voltaire plays this role in the fashion of Groucho Marx." I invited Stadlen to substitute another harmless, lecherous vaudevillean for Groucho, and he came up with Irwin Corey.

Other places in the script I characterized the Governor as Errol Flynn, and so Stadlen wears an Errol Flynn wig and a tatty Errol Flynn uniform. I arranged a reading of the play with a provisional cast, which included Mark and Maureen, Sam Freed, whom I'd picked for Maximilian, and June Gable, whom I had asked to read the Old Lady. It went even better than our fondest dreams, with Stadlen, adding an impersonation of Mel Brooks's Oldest Man in the World, as the Tibetan Monk.

In the meantime, unbeknownst to me, Julie Newmar signed to do a play for Joseph Papp. Problem solved.

Soon after we had signed Lewis Stadlen, Roscoe Lee

Browne called to ask what was happening with *Candide*. He had no knowledge of his agent's refusal on his behalf. That is not unusual.

At this point I sat down with Steve Sondheim to discuss new lyrics. We needed an opening number to introduce four of the leading characters of the play in a humorous way, to set a lightly cynical, informal tone for the show, and to establish the sensuality and the innocence of the people.

Hugh wrote a monologue for Voltaire designed to orient the audience to the time and place, and four vignettes, some of which Steve set to Bernstein's music from the Venice "Gavotte" and called "Life Is Happiness Indeed."

The first quatrain is Candide's and illustrates how to tell an audience quickly where it's going.

> *(Candide is discovered on a hillock,*
> *an angry falcon perched on his left*
> *wrist)*
>> Life is happiness indeed:
>> Mares to ride and books to read.
>> Though of noble birth I'm not,
>> I'm delighted with my lot.
>
>> Though I've no distinctive features
>> And I've no official mother
>> I love all my fellow creatures
>> And the creatures love each other.
> *(He releases the falcon, which is*
> *jerked clumsily from his wrist and*
> *shoots upward stiffly to disappear.*
> *A second later a large stuffed swan*
> *clunks down on the stage)*

Cunégonde sings about the beautiful rosebush she's tending:

> Life is happiness indeed:
> I have everything I need.
> I am rich and unattached
> And my beauty is unmatched.
>
> With the rose my only rival
> I admit to some frustration;
> What a pity its survival
> Is of limited duration.*
>
> *(In a fit of jealousy, she tears
> one of the roses from its branch)*

And so on. In each instance, the aftertaste.

In addition to the opening, we resurrected a Fons Pietatis, which Bernstein had written for the original.

Latouche and Bernstein had written "What a Lovely Day for an Auto da Fé," which became one of our "big" production numbers. We needed some solo lyrics in the middle section for spectators, and Sondheim provided those.

Sondheim also wrote a lament for Candide, using the Paris "Mazurka."

We had to find a substitution for the song "Eldorado," something funny, something for two pink sheep and a lion to sing. Eldorado figures importantly in the novel, describing a perfect society where human beings wilt from boredom. There was nothing wrong with the original "Eldo-

---

* Copyright © 1973 By Beautiful Music Inc.
Revelation Music Publishing Co.

rado" except that they had chosen to bypass Eldorado and we had chosen to visit it. Bernstein had written a lovely melody in 1956, "Fernando's Lullaby," and Steve set a lyric to it.

When we reexamined the script, in our efforts to keep everything moving, the sameness of pace was boring. We had to find places to stop for breath. The need to slow things down prompted a series of questions by Candide of a disembodied Voltaire. These questions and Voltaire's replies anchor the evening.

So much for the new material.

We went into rehearsal on October 21. I cautioned the young company not to turn our set into a gymnasium. This was not to be an evening with a stopwatch, not to be about racing and jumping and shouting and sweating, mindless aiming to please. If ever there was a show to which "less is more" applied, *Candide* would be it.

And subsequently, the few problems we had with performance involved effort—or rather, effort showing. I predicted that the environment, which was the show, was as off-putting as it was engaging. Just as many people were going to label it avant-garde hijinks on wooden boards. To counter that, we must respect the content, the structure, the rhythms, that Hugh had carefully provided. Vitality would follow effortlessly.

To protect myself, I scheduled six and a half weeks of rehearsals before the first preview. Pat Birch and I staged the show in eight days. Still, it had its advantages. If we had a sluggish day, we let it go. If things were going well, we worked a full five hours and quit. We rarely bothered to break for lunch—avoided coming back logy and distracted. If someone's voice was bothering him, he saved it. One of our girls was mugged on the second day of rehearsal. When she came back, it was good to see her, but her absence hadn't pressed us.

I began to appreciate the privileges of socialized theatre, the seven months that Dr. Walter Felsenstein required to direct *Fiddler on the Roof* in East Berlin. (I'm only kidding; given that time, I would go nuts.)

Also, we had the luxury of four weeks to try it on small groups of friends. Based on their responses, we kept filling and building. *Candide* evolved.

One of the things that made it all so much fun was that I was not worrying about returning an investment. I was not worrying about it running indefinitely. I was doing a show for five weeks in Brooklyn.

We opened over a ten-day period with critics at every performance. We were sold out beforehand and the Brooklyn run was extended two weeks. The reviews were marvelous, many suggesting a move to Broadway, the *Times* concerned that we might lose something in the course of it.

Now let's talk about how not to produce a show. Let's talk about how I ignored everything I'd learned, or should have learned.

Kalfin and his partners, Michael David and Burl Hash, Howard Haines, Ruth Mitchell, and I set out in search of space in Manhattan, preferably a ballroom. The available ballrooms are in old hotels and too small to contain us. The set in Brooklyn required a room at least sixty by forty feet. In order to increase the capacity of the audience, we needed more than that. The larger hotels weren't interested. We couldn't compete with conventions.

Haines, my general manager, canvassed the City Center basement, an abandoned bowling alley, and for a time seemed to be doing business with the Waldorf Astoria for the Sert Room.

Always in the back of my mind was the possibility of the Broadway or Winter Garden Theatres, of stripping them of their seats and utilizing the space on their vast stages for a portion of our audience. Both theatres were available.

The Winter Garden would have been easier because its balcony is small, wasting less of the usable space on the orchestra floor, but it is a more sought-after theatre, and I reasoned the Shuberts would not give us a contract to insure an indefinite run.

The Broadway, something of a white elephant, is a good theatre. Not as handsome as the Winter Garden, and a couple of blocks further up on Broadway, it is abutted by a rather ugly parking lot and surrounded by steadily declining real estate. Paradoxically, that was an advantage to us. I did not underestimate the ambiance of the Brooklyn Academy of Music, of its faded elegant lobby, even more, of the fourth floor, where the Chelsea is. I coveted the ingratiating informality, the earnestness of its tatty peeling walls and threadbare carpets. I joked that there was even an additional thrill getting from the Atlantic Avenue subway station to the Academy of Music alive! Perhaps we would simulate that on Broadway and Fifty-third Street.

The economics of the production in Brooklyn were such that at capacity the Chelsea Theatre Center lost $4000 a week. When they extended the run two weeks, that represented a sacrifice of $8000. However, in order to move to

Broadway (where they might realize some profits), we had to keep the weeks between the closing in Brooklyn and the opening on Broadway to a minimum.

What did moving quickly incur? Kalfin and I told the cast the good news, which was met with a great whoop of joy, and then the negotiating began. Billing, never a factor before, and television "out clauses" tended to give the lie to the original concept, which is that it was a group effort. All these things I understand. I understand how hazardous and frustrating an actor's life can be. The irony is simply that within minutes of the decision, the air surrounding the project was changing.

That was just the beginning, and the actors were the least of it.

Next we met with the architects, as well as Eugene Lee, to determine how to preserve the structure and increase the size of the audience observing the show. We figured the move to cost a couple of hundred thousand dollars, including building, advertising, and one week's rehearsal. The new structure had to qualify from the point of view of Fire and Building Department regulations, more rigorous in a Broadway theatre than they would have been in a ballroom.

We started to blueprint a production which would accommodate, we hoped, 1000 people against the 180 in Brooklyn, and at the same time, preserve the original playing areas. We succeeded with the latter. The Broadway playing area is twenty feet longer than the one in Brooklyn, but the stages are identical.

To add capacity we created "the bleachers," on a first-come, first-served basis, and I moved the show into the bleachers whenever possible.

Instead of 1000 seats, we settled for 900.

Simultaneously we petitioned the Musicians Local 802. Ordinarily the Broadway (capacity 1800) by contract must carry a minimum of twenty-five musicians. With *Candide* at the Broadway (capacity 900), we requested an adjustment to reflect the new capacity. At a hearing before the union's Executive Board, I pointed out that in Brooklyn, according to that contract, we might have done the show with one pianist, but instead we had chosen to use thirteen musicians.

The score had been orchestrated for thirteen musicians and we hoped to transfer them to New York. With a capacity of 900 *Candide* was a risky proposition. It would take a minimum of forty weeks to return its investment, but once it had, it represented a chance for the Chelsea to see some money. Twenty-five musicians and necessary re-orchestrations would delay that.

They rejected our petition.

It was too late to turn back. We had closed in Brooklyn on January 20, and in order to reopen without losing momentum, we were obliged to sign the Broadway Theatre contract, move ahead with the architects, and spend money advertising our plan while awaiting the union's decision. It never occurred to me they would turn us down.

We requested a second hearing, this time before the Musical Theatre Committee of the union. It was pointed out by Gerald Schoenfeld of the Shubert Organization that the Broadway Theatre had been empty for thirteen months (excepting one night for the Miss U.S.A. Pageant), that we were bringing in a hit musical which might run there indefinitely, providing we could keep the operating expenses within sensible limits. Ruth Mitchell informed them that there would be other productions, if the show succeeded on Broadway—in Los Angeles, Boston, and so on—giving jobs to musicians (of course, from other locals!).

The union turned *them* down.

It is interesting that when the musicians' union turned us down the second time, the stagehands' union called and offered to intervene. They did and it didn't work.

There was a third hearing, at which time the musicians' union ruled that while twenty-five musicians were mandatory, we would not have to pay them extra for wearing funny hats and vests while playing (ordinarily they get about $68 a week more for that).

Three weeks had gone by and it was too late to cancel the show. We decided we could not afford to reorchestrate; consequently, there are twenty-five musicians on the payroll, eighteen of whom play, while seven sit in the basement.

I wrote the union.

January 28, 1974

Mr. Max Aarons, President
American Federation of Musicians
Local 802
261 West 52nd Street
New York City 10019

Gentlemen:

I can't repress the desire to tell you how insulting I thought the behavior accorded me at the meeting I was invited to attend before the Executive Board of Local 802.

It is unprecedented in my twenty years as an active producer of musicals to have met with so little knowledge of not only what I do in the theatre, but what is done by my peers.

We approached you to aid us in making a production viable on Broadway so that it can relight a theatre which has been closed for over a year and perhaps give employment to musicians, actors, stagehands, wardrobe women, etc., here and across the country. The rudeness, the outright suspicion, with which our request for practical help was met prompts me to make the following statement.

Personally, I have made my first and last appearance before your august board. Also whenever possible—and I think it will be possible more often than not—I will seek to design my future productions for the smaller theatres. The lack of logic that motivated your final decision to force us to use 25 musicians in a theatre with a seating capacity of 900 bears out my worst fears, that the theatre is not dying: rather, it is being systematically killed.

Sincerely,
Harold Prince

HP:am
CC: Gerald Schoenfeld

(How can I feel this way about people who play the violin!)

Isn't it possible that we are reaching a time when unions must assume a responsibility for the future of the theatre? Is it too much to suggest that a committee of last resort be established from among the producers, the artists, the craft unions to deal expeditiously with problems that affect the entire industry? This committee should be headed by an impartial figure with some political and public-relations experience, but more important, someone whose stature would command respect from the individual guilds and unions.

Surely the collaboration of artists to create a play is an

impossible concept, but it works. Why, then, cannot groups of the same artists collaborate to the benefit of all?

I had problems with Equity as well. In the Broadway we found that because of the choreography, the actors could not be heard singing Sondheim's solo lines in the "Auto da Fé." I phoned Equity the day before we opened and asked for permission to tape those eight lines during a performance without paying each of the actors a week's salary. (At this point we were $100,000 over budget.) I was informed that the Equity Council was not meeting until the following week. By that time we would be open. I urged them to make an exception. They turned me down. I went back to the theatre and cut the two quatrains, and Pat Birch pieced the number together.

The move to Broadway became the responsibility, more than anyone else, of Howard Haines, working with the architect (Leslie Armstrong of Armstrong, Childs and Associates, who had supervised the musical *Dude* a year earlier in the same theatre), a consulting engineer (Henry M. Garsson), and the builder (Peter Feller). I never saw *Dude,* but we benefited from the experience of that production in money, time, and, one hopes, wear and tear on the nerves, but I can't imagine being *more* apprehensive than I was in the seven-week period during which we reconstructed the interior of the Broadway to the specifications of the city agencies.

No sooner had we accommodated their rules, but I would come into the theatre and eliminate seats. One day I took out 121 in the bleacher section because of sightlines. The point is, with *Candide,* no one in the audience sees everything, but everyone must see almost everything.

There's no question but that we couldn't have gotten *Candide* on without Peter Feller's help. Over those seven weeks he would no sooner get the structure up when he would have to change it. Raise this row, take out these seats, raise that stage, put backs on those benches, guardrails along that aisle, and so on.

By the time we were ready for Tharon Musser, she had two and a half days to light the show.

At the Chelsea there was no amplification. On Broadway the problems were critical. We brought Jack Mann over from *Night Music* to solve them. Five minutes before we opened the doors for our first performance Tharon was adjusting specials, Jack was concealing shotgun microphones (a patron refused to sit next to one of them, explaining that she likes to talk during a show), Howard Haines was still numbering seats, and I was rehearsing the ushers.

Adjusting *Candide* to the Broadway was more like opening a new hotel than a play (Are the elevators working? How is room service?).

I had anticipated some problems acclimating the audience to an unfamiliar environment, but it was far worse than I imagined. Coming in off Broadway, under a conventional marquee, into a conventional lobby, the structure frightened them. There is a book, *The Hidden Dimension*, by Edward Hall, which deals in detail with the amount of space an individual requires in order to feel secure. It differs with the individual. It is an instinct shared by animals. There is a Spanish word, *querencia*, which defines the space around the bull which he needs to remain passive. When the bullfighter violates that space, the bull charges.

Our audience charged, some refusing seat locations, complaining about sightlines, maximizing the discomforts of grandstand seating. An environment which would have been acceptable to them in a ball park offended them in a theatre.

So the Chelsea redecorated the lobby, covered the marble floor with unfinished plywood, set up hot-dog-and-beer stands, hung balloons and streamers and the canvas drops from the Chelsea production to obliterate the crystal chandeliers and the gold leaf. Then Michael David designed an advertising campaign defining the *Candide* person. The *Candide* person buys a can of beer and fills his pockets with free peanuts on the way in. He sits on a wooden bench with a back or in the pit on a padded stool. If he can't see something, he rises in his seat. If he's in the pit, he turns 360 degrees to catch the action. It worked.

Now that you can *see* from the seats and there are pads on them, and backs on all but those in the pit (and the bleachers), I assumed the complaint letters would stop coming in. They haven't. Not entirely. And that is because so much of the Broadway audience today is corrupt, concerned with creature comforts, rejecting the experience. If you gave those people beds, they could come in and sleep and we wouldn't have to worry about what we put up on the stage.

Part of the blame is ours for desensitizing them, but if the theatre is to be a collaboration of living beings on either side of the proscenium, then they are derelict in their responsibilities.

Earlier I have said that each play seeds the next. Nowhere is it more apparent than with the success of *Candide*.

I have known for years that content dictates form, but in *Baker Street* I didn't have the courage to go full distance with the form, and in *Zorba* I tried to twist the content to fit the form. In *Candide* form and content merged easily.

It occurs to me that I loved working on *Candide* in Brooklyn and I hated bringing it to Broadway.

I must conclude from this that I am growing older, the wear and tear on the nerves is more difficult to take. Is it possible that explains why so many theatre artists seem to retire in their forties or move away from directing or writing for the theatre into a more solitary creative experience?

Or, and this is just as likely, maybe I simply don't enjoy producing.

CHAPTER 27

The following afterthoughts don't belong in any particular chapter. Still, they seem worth recording;

For the present my investors subsidize me. With costs spiraling, how long will that continue? Eventually commercial theatre will be subsidized by the National Endowment and individual foundations. Just imagine, had a foundation been half-owner of *Fiddler,* how many productions those profits would have financed. I recognize the stigma attached to such thinking, but perhaps the successful alliance of the Chelsea and my office will change things.

Benefit audiences used to be dangerous. They tended to clutter the aisles with sociability. And when the curtain went up, they turned apathetic and resentful of the price they had paid. But times have changed. They have acquired taste. The tickets are in part tax-deductible. The audiences have seen more shows and become more discriminating. Also, they are more polite. Maybe they are enjoying themselves.

The newspaper fellows who spend their lives extolling the freedom of nonprofit theatre have no idea how much more freedom there can be in the commercial theatre. All the politicking, campaigning in behalf of money. I sometimes wonder where is the marketplace and who are the merchants.

I am encouraged by the programs which speak to enlarging the theatre audience. Maybe it takes a real crisis. Anyway, the Theatre Development Fund's ticket booth has had tremendous affect on the business. I wish that producers with smash hits would make even a token allotment of seats. It is shortsighted not to have every attraction represented in the Times Square Booth.

There are those who miss the traditional opening night with all its glamor and dress-up. Weighed against the self-consciousness of perennial opening-nighters who don't go to theatre on any other night, anxious and overfriendly investors, and the press, I still prefer four openings with seats sold to the general public at the box office. Also, it forces the cast to pace itself and give a more natural performance.

I don't think the plan to pay off plays on tour before opening on Broadway is going to work. Touring isn't good for shows. The scenery, the costumes, and the actors wear out. More accurately, it is difficult for an actor to manage eight performances on tour and five hours of extensive rehearsal every day for a prolonged period. In addition, most of the new theatres on the road are too large to *fix* in.

The theatre has become overly reliant on lawyers and agents. I find myself reminding them that with a hit you make a lot of money. Don't squeeze it dry. Leave something in it for the investors.

The only thing interesting to me in Pauline Kael's review of the *Fiddler* film is a sentence in which she said she'd never seen the play. How in hell can a person in the business of reviewing ignore the most esteemed works in the allied arts? Is it too much to ask that film critics visit the theatre and vice versa? That all critics visit museums and lecture halls and turn on their television sets? Pauline Kael should have seen the play. She had seven and a half years to see it.

The trouble with so many of the creative people on Broadway is that they don't read, they don't travel, they don't inform themselves. They are so talented and undereducated. In the regions they tend to be more educated than talented.

At the Film Festival in San Francisco (October 1971), I was asked why I didn't direct the film versions of the musicals I had done. I replied I don't like movie musicals: I think there is a contradiction in terms.

I don't think you can make a creative person out of someone who isn't one. But I think you can encourage someone who has it buried so deeply inside that he might not get to it.

It has taken years, but the unions have finally agreed to permit the filming of theatrical performances to be kept in the Lincoln Center Library. Why should that have taken years!

It occurs to me on rereading this book that I have neglected (avoided) describing the intangible aspects of the creative process, the private and exhilarating experience which either defies illumination, or probably more accurately, desires privacy. There is a muse and it is mystical. Call it intuition. Let it go at that.

About two years ago John Weidman, a law student at Yale, brought me the outline for a play about Commodore Perry's visit to Japan. It was realistic, in the style of the *Caine Mutiny Court-Martial.* Not the sort of theatre I care for. I suggested instead that he tell the story as though it were written by a Japanese playwright in the Kabuki style, with the Americans the traditional Kabuki villains. He has done that and called it *Pacific Overtures.* It will be a musical. Steve Sondheim is writing the score; Pat Birch will choreograph, Boris is designing the scenery, and Florence Klotz the costumes. It comes next.

No, the next one is for the Phoenix: Congreve's *Love for Love.* We go into rehearsal on Labor Day. I usually

return from Europe the day before and go to work on the
holiday. It's quiet, the phones don't ring, and the trans-
portation is easy.

1974
New York City

Appendix A

THE PAJAMA GAME

OPENING: May 13, 1954, St. James Theatre
CLOSING: November 24, 1956
NUMBER OF PERFORMANCES: 1060
BOOK BY George Abbott AND Richard Bissell
MUSIC AND LYRICS BY Richard Adler AND Jerry Ross
SCENERY AND COSTUMES BY Lemuel Ayers
CHOREOGRAPHY BY Bob Fosse
PRODUCTION DIRECTED BY George Abbott AND Jerome Robbins
PRODUCED BY Frederick Brisson, Robert E. Griffith, AND Harold
    S. Prince

DAMN YANKEES

OPENING: May 5, 1955, 46th Street Theater
CLOSING: October 12, 1957
NUMBER OF PERFORMANCES: 1012
BOOK BY George Abbott AND Douglass Wallop
MUSIC AND LYRICS BY Richard Adler AND Jerry Ross
DANCES AND MUSICAL NUMBERS STAGED BY Bob Fosse
SCENERY AND COSTUMES DESIGNED BY William AND Jean Eckart

PRODUCTION DIRECTED BY George Abbott
PRODUCED BY Frederick Brisson, Robert E. Griffith, AND Harold
S. Prince (IN ASSOCIATION WITH Albert B. Taylor)

NEW GIRL IN TOWN

OPENING: May 14, 1957, 46th Street Theater
CLOSING: May 24, 1958
NUMBER OF PERFORMANCES: 439
BOOK BY George Abbott
MUSIC AND LYRICS BY Bob Merrill
DANCES AND MUSICAL NUMBERS STAGED BY Bob Fosse
PRODUCTION DESIGNED BY Rouben Ter-Arutunian
PRODUCTION DIRECTED BY George Abbott
PRODUCED BY Frederick Brisson, Robert E. Griffith, AND Harold
S. Prince

WEST SIDE STORY

OPENING: September 26, 1957, Winter Garden Theatre
CLOSING: June 27, 1959
NUMBER OF PERFORMANCES: 772
REOPENING: April 27, 1960, Winter Garden Theatre
RECLOSING: December 10, 1960
NUMBER OF PERFORMANCES: 253
BOOK BY Arthur Laurents
MUSIC BY Leonard Bernstein
LYRICS BY Stephen Sondheim
SCENIC PRODUCTION BY Oliver Smith
COSTUMES DESIGNED BY Irene Sharaff
LIGHTING BY Jean Rosenthal
ENTIRE PRODUCTION DIRECTED AND CHOREOGRAPHED BY Jerome
Robbins
CO-CHOREOGRAPHER, Peter Gennaro
PRODUCED BY Robert E. Griffith AND Harold S. Prince (BY AR-
RANGEMENT WITH Roger L. Stevens)

Appendix A

A SWIM IN THE SEA

OPENING: September 15, 1958 (Philadelphia)
CLOSING: September 27, 1958 (Philadelphia)
NUMBER OF PERFORMANCES: 16
BOOK BY Jess Gregg
SCENERY AND LIGHTING BY James Riley
COSTUMES BY Hazel Roy
DIRECTED BY Elliott Silverstein
PRODUCED BY Robert E. Griffith AND Harold S. Prince

FIORELLO!

OPENING: November 23, 1959, Broadhurst Theatre
CLOSING: October 28, 1961
NUMBER OF PERFORMANCES: 800
BOOK BY Jerome Weidman AND George Abbott
MUSIC BY Jerry Bock
LYRICS BY Sheldon Harnick
CHOREOGRAPHY BY Peter Gennaro
SCENERY, COSTUMES AND LIGHTING DESIGNED BY William AND
    Jean Eckart
PRODUCTION DIRECTED BY George Abbott
PRODUCED BY Robert E. Griffith AND Harold S. Prince

TENDERLOIN

OPENING: October 17, 1960, 46th Street Theater
CLOSING: April 22, 1961
NUMBER OF PERFORMANCES: 214
BOOK BY George Abbott AND Jerome Weidman
MUSIC BY Jerry Bock
LYRICS BY Sheldon Harnick
DANCES AND MUSICAL NUMBERS STAGED BY Joe Layton
SETS AND COSTUMES BY Cecil Beaton
PRODUCTION DIRECTED BY George Abbott
PRODUCED BY Robert E. Griffith AND Harold S. Prince

A CALL ON KUPRIN

OPENING: May 25, 1961, Broadhurst Theatre
CLOSING: June 3, 1961
NUMBER OF PERFORMANCES: 14
BOOK BY Jerome Lawrence AND Robert E. Lee
SETTINGS BY Donald Oenslager
COSTUMES BY Florence Klotz
DIRECTED BY George Abbott
PRODUCED BY Robert E. Griffith AND Harold S. Prince

TAKE HER, SHE'S MINE

OPENING: December 21, 1961, Biltmore Theatre
CLOSING: December 8, 1962
NUMBER OF PERFORMANCES: 404
BOOK BY Phoebe AND Henry Ephron
SCENERY AND LIGHTING BY William AND Jean Eckart
COSTUMES BY Florence Klotz
DIRECTED BY George Abbott
PRODUCED BY Harold S. Prince

A FAMILY AFFAIR

OPENING: January 27, 1962, Billy Rose Theatre
CLOSING: March 25, 1962
NUMBER OF PERFORMANCES: 65
BOOK BY James Goldman, John Kander, AND William Goldman
DIRECTED BY Harold Prince
CHOREOGRAPHY BY John Butler
MUSICAL NUMBERS STAGED BY Bob Herget
SETTINGS AND LIGHTING BY David Hays
COSTUMES DESIGNED BY Robert Fletcher
PRODUCED BY Andrew Siff

A FUNNY THING HAPPENED ON THE WAY TO THE FORUM

OPENING: May 8, 1962, Alvin Theatre
CLOSING: August 29, 1964
NUMBER OF PERFORMANCES: 975
BOOK BY Burt Shevelove AND Larry Gelbart
MUSIC AND LYRICS BY Stephen Sondheim
CHOREOGRAPHY AND MUSICAL STAGING BY Jack Cole
SETTINGS AND COSTUMES BY Tony Walton
LIGHTING BY Jean Rosenthal
PRODUCTION DIRECTED BY George Abbott
PRODUCED BY Harold Prince

SHE LOVES ME

OPENING: April 23, 1963, Eugene O'Neill Theatre
CLOSING: January 11, 1964
NUMBER OF PERFORMANCES: 303
BOOK BY Joe Masteroff
MUSIC BY Jerry Bock
LYRICS BY Sheldon Harnick
MUSICAL NUMBERS STAGED BY Carol Haney
SETTINGS AND LIGHTING BY William AND Jean Eckart
COSTUMES BY Patricia Zipprodt
PRODUCTION DIRECTED BY Harold Prince
PRODUCED BY Harold Prince (IN ASSOCIATION WITH Lawrence N. Kasha AND Philip C. McKenna)

FIDDLER ON THE ROOF

OPENING: September 22, 1964, Imperial Theatre
CLOSING: July 2, 1972
NUMBER OF PERFORMANCES: 3242
BOOK BY Joseph Stein
MUSIC BY Jerry Bock

Lyrics by Sheldon Harnick
Entire Production Directed and Choreographed by Jerome Robbins
Settings by Boris Aronson
Costumes by Patricia Zipprodt
Lighting by Jean Rosenthal
Produced by Harold Prince

BAKER STREET

Opening: February 16, 1965, Broadway Theatre
Closing: November 14, 1965
Number of Performances: 313
Book by Jerome Coopersmith
Music and Lyrics by Marian Grudeff and Raymond Jessel
Choreography by Lee Becker Theodore
Production designed by Oliver Smith
Lighting by Jean Rosenthal
Production Directed by Harold Prince
Produced by Alexander H. Cohen

POOR BITOS

Opening: November 14, 1964, Cort Theatre
Closing: November 28, 1964
Number of Performances: 17
A Play by Jean Anouilh
Translated by Lucienne Hill
Foreign Production Designed by Timothy O'Brien
American Production Supervised by Jean Rosenthal
Costumes by Donald Brooks
Lighting by Jean Rosenthal
Directed by Shirley Butler
Produced by Harold Prince (in association with Michael Codron and Pledon Ltd.)

Appendix A

FLORA, THE RED MENACE

OPENING: May 11, 1965, Alvin Theatre
CLOSING: July 24, 1965
NUMBER OF PERFORMANCES: 85
BOOK BY George Abbott AND Robert Russell
MUSIC BY John Kander
LYRICS BY Fred Ebb
DANCE AND MUSICAL NUMBERS STAGED BY Lee Theodore
SETTINGS BY William AND Jean Eckart
COSTUMES BY Donald Brooks
LIGHTING BY Tharon Musser
PRODUCTION DIRECTED BY George Abbott
PRODUCED BY Harold Prince

"IT'S A BIRD . . . IT'S A PLANE . . . IT'S SUPERMAN"

OPENING: March 29, 1966, Alvin Theatre
CLOSING: July 17, 1966
NUMBER OF PERFORMANCES: 128
MUSIC BY Charles Strouse
LYRICS BY Lee Adams
BOOK BY David Newman AND Robert Benton
SCENERY AND LIGHTING BY Robert Randolph
COSTUMES BY Florence Klotz
DANCES AND MUSICAL NUMBERS STAGED BY Ernest Flatt
PRODUCTION DIRECTED BY Harold Prince
PRODUCED BY Harold Prince (IN ASSOCIATION WITH Ruth Mitchell)

CABARET

OPENING: November 20, 1966, Broadhurst Theatre
CLOSING: September 6, 1969
NUMBER OF PERFORMANCES: 1166
BOOK BY Joe Masteroff

MUSIC BY John Kander
LYRICS BY Fred Ebb
DANCES AND CABARET NUMBERS BY Ronald Field
SCENERY BY Boris Aronson
COSTUMES BY Patricia Zipprodt
LIGHTING BY Jean Rosenthal
PRODUCTION DIRECTED BY Harold Prince
PRODUCED BY Harold Prince (IN ASSOCIATION WITH Ruth Mitchell)

ZORBA

OPENING: November 17, 1968, Imperial Theatre
CLOSING: August 9, 1969
NUMBER OF PERFORMANCES: 305
BOOK BY Joseph Stein
MUSIC BY John Kander
LYRICS BY Fred Ebb
CHOREOGRAPHY BY Ronald Field
SCENIC PRODUCTION DESIGNED BY Boris Aronson
COSTUMES BY Patricia Zipprodt
LIGHTING BY Richard Pilbrow
PRODUCTION DIRECTED BY Harold Prince
PRODUCED BY Harold Prince (IN ASSOCIATION WITH Ruth Mitchell)

COMPANY

OPENING: April 26, 1970, Alvin Theatre
CLOSING: January 1, 1972
NUMBER OF PERFORMANCES: 706
MUSIC AND LYRICS BY Stephen Sondheim
BOOK BY George Furth
SETS AND PROJECTIONS DESIGNED BY Boris Aronson
COSTUMES BY D. D. Ryan
LIGHTING BY Robert Ornbo

Appendix A

MUSICAL NUMBERS STAGED BY Michael Bennett
PRODUCTION DIRECTED BY Harold Prince
PRODUCED BY Harold Prince (IN ASSOCIATION WITH Ruth Mitchell)

FOLLIES

OPENING: April 4, 1971, Winter Garden Theatre
CLOSING: July 1, 1972
NUMBER OF PERFORMANCES: 522
MUSIC AND LYRICS BY Stephen Sondheim
BOOK BY James Goldman
SCENIC PRODUCTION DESIGNED BY Boris Aronson
COSTUMES BY Florence Klotz
LIGHTING BY Tharon Musser
Choreography BY Michael Bennett
PRODUCTION DIRECTED BY Harold Prince AND Michael Bennett
PRODUCED BY Harold Prince (IN ASSOCIATION WITH Ruth Mitchell)

A LITTLE NIGHT MUSIC

OPENING: February 25, 1973, Shubert Theatre
CLOSING: August 3, 1974
NUMBER OF PERFORMANCES: 601
MUSIC AND LYRICS BY Stephen Sondheim
BOOK BY Hugh Wheeler
CHOREOGRAPHY BY Patricia Birch
SCENIC PRODUCTION DESIGNED BY Boris Aronson
COSTUMES BY Florence Klotz
LIGHTING BY Tharon Musser
PRODUCTION DIRECTED BY Harold Prince
PRODUCED BY Harold Prince (IN ASSOCIATION WITH Ruth Mitchell)

CANDIDE (Broadway)

OPENING: March 5, 1974, Broadway Theatre
CLOSING:
NUMBER OF PERFORMANCES:
MUSIC COMPOSED BY Leonard Bernstein
BOOK ADAPTED FROM Voltaire BY Hugh Wheeler
LYRICS BY Richard Wilbur
ADDITIONAL LYRICS BY Stephen Sondheim AND John Latouche
LIGHTING DESIGNED BY Tharon Musser
SETS AND COSTUMES DESIGNED BY Eugene AND Franne Lee
CHOREOGRAPHED BY Patricia Birch
DIRECTED BY Harold Prince
PRODUCED BY THE CHELSEA THEATER CENTER OF BROOKLYN
    (IN CONJUNCTION WITH Harold Prince AND Ruth Mitchell)

Appendix B

The Prince production record as of September 1, 1974

Show	Season	Capital	Profit or Loss to Backers
* THE PAJAMA GAME	1953–54	$250,000	$972,500 profit
* DAMN YANKEES	1954–55	$250,000	$643,750 profit
NEW GIRL IN TOWN	1956–57	$300,000	$72,250 profit
* WEST SIDE STORY	1957–58	$300,000	$1,090,000 profit
A SWIM IN THE SEA (Closed in Philadelphia)	1957–58	$100,000	$48,000 loss
* FIORELLO!	1959–60	$300,000	$265,500 profit
TENDERLOIN	1960–61	$350,000	$92,400 loss
A CALL ON KUPRIN	1960–61	$150,000	$150,000 loss
* TAKE HER, SHE'S MINE	1961–62	$150,000	$46,125 profit
* A FUNNY THING HAPPENED ON THE WAY TO THE FORUM	1961–62	$300,000	$377,000 profit
SHE LOVES ME	1962–63	$300,000	$239,250 loss
* FIDDLER ON THE ROOF	1964–65	$375,000	$4,552,500 profit
POOR BITOS	1964–65	$90,000	$90,000 loss
FLORA, THE RED MENACE	1964–65	$400,000	$381,000 loss
SUPERMAN	1965–66	$400,000	$400,000 loss
* CABARET	1966–67	$500,000	$1,017,500 profit
* ZORBA	1968–69	$500,000	$131,250 loss
* COMPANY	1969–70	$550,000	$56,000 profit
* FOLLIES	1970–71	$700,000	$665,000 loss
* A LITTLE NIGHT MUSIC	1972–73	$650,000	$97,500 profit
* CANDIDE (opened March 5, 1974)	1973–74	$450,000	

* Indicates production is still earning income.

INDEX

Index

Index

Index

Index

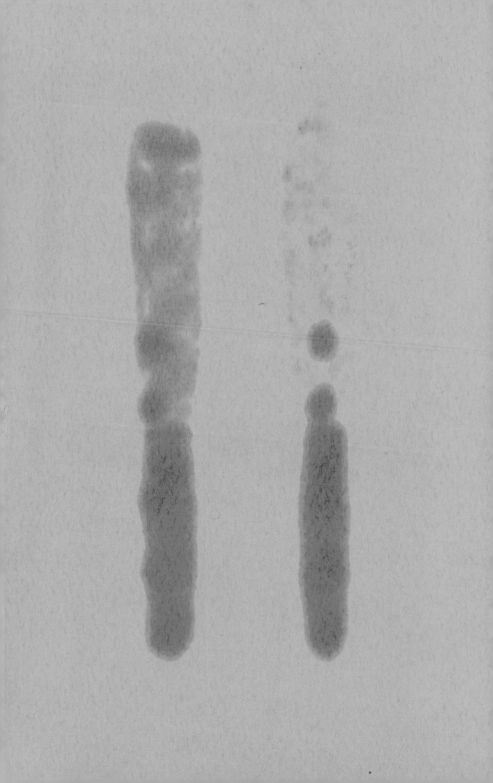